THE S

Cultivating Authority

JESSICA ONSAGA

This series is dedicated to the sons of God who will say "YES" to Yahweh no matter the cost. May these books help you grow in sonship and maturity in your walk with Christ.

The Sonship Series: Cultivating Authority

Jessica Onsaga

Copyright © 2023

Published by Seraph Creative

www.seraphcreative.org

TABLE OF CONTENTS

FOREWORD

A heart surrendered in unwavering devotion to Jesus wields power beyond measure. As we delve deeper into the art of romancing the King through our steadfast focus, a realm of authority beyond the ordinary unfolds—a realm where devotion becomes a channel for profound empowerment.

From this posture of heart, our union with Jesus becomes the central experience from which we live. This is the way into a life of experiencing Christ within. Here we become secure in His love, able to trust and rest, and over time, anything other than His truth begins to seem illogical.

This is the life Jessica has chosen and through her deepening intimacy with Jesus, has received revelation and wisdom from the heart of God that has healed and transformed her life. As the scripture tells us in Ephesians 4:23-24, she has been changed by every unfolding revelation and has been transformed as she has embraced the glorious Christ within as her new life, and now lives in union with Him.

Jessica has chosen the better way; the life of devotion, of full dependency on Jesus, and has tasted the freedom and authority that becomes ours as we trust Him with everything and live life according to the ways of His heart. Her courage and vulnerability, opening her life with Jesus to us through the pages of this profound book, has provided real hope for each one of us. 'Cultivating Authority' will show you what's possible and will provide you with keys to know how! Read slowly, with the eyes of your heart on the King. You were born for this hour; to live a deep life of authentic, uninterrupted intimacy where God's heart is open to you and entrusted to you, and where you become an overflowing vessel of His beauty, power and glory!

"Now you are ready, my bride, to come with me as we climb the highest peaks together. Come with me through the archway of trust." Song of Songs 4:8 TPT

Liz Wright
Founder & CEO of the International Mentoring Community
International Best Selling Author of Reflecting God and Loved
Presenter of Encountering God on God TV & host of Live Your
Best Life with Charisma Podcast Network

TESTIMONIALS

I am thrilled to have read this book series! I grew up in church, but when life happened, and I found myself in a major struggle, tormented in my mind by the enemy... my church didn't know how to help me. They were going through the motions of religion but didn't know how to connect to Abba. I went searching for the powerful God I'd read about, hoping for help, but it took almost 2 decades before I found a church that taught me some useful tools. But I was still struggling with that one big issue. Like Moses and the Israelites wandering in circles in the wilderness, I was tired of going around the same mountain again and again.

One year ago, my big struggle showed up again, and it happened right as I was reading this series. I was so relieved to read about the tools Jessica so clearly laid out in the books! They were exactly what I needed! She has a way of putting everything so simply, broken down into bite-sized pieces that can be easily applied right away. It's all about Jesus and relationship with Him, but even that simple statement can feel difficult when the enemy is in an all-out attack. I found the tools easy to understand and utilize, and I began to see progress like never before! It's not an instant fix, but Jessica has a beautiful way of encouraging us about the process. After a long rough season, this past year has been one of the best in my life! I'm seeing victories in my big struggle, and freedom is finally in sight! I am so incredibly grateful for Jessica's teachings in my life, and I know that many others will be blessed through this series.

--Jessi Osborne

I was saved in the county jail on the 13th day of May 2007, and I immediately fell in love with the Lord. Or so I thought. What started out as a search for the truth, wound up leading me into torment, for I started adopting religion at an almost inconceivable rate over the next 12 years. One day I decided that this wasn't working. The enemy had me believing all his lies instead of me getting the truth that I so desperately needed: I needed a deep abiding relationship with the One who died so that I could walk in Freedom. I was so wound up in religiosity, that I didn't know which way to turn. After I got out of prison in March of 2023, I found the truth while reading a book called The Foundation (Book 1 of the Sonship Series). This book and series led me to the Words of Truth that Jesus wanted me to hear, and they took hold of my heart. As I searched these Words of Truth, I actually came to the knowledge that I could have a deep abiding relationship with my Savior. Jessica's books started me on my journey for the Voice of Truth. I'm beginning to understand these foundational truths that I have missed over the last 15 years. I'm finally learning how to love Jesus like I wanted to all my life, and I'm also learning to allow him to love me. This deep, abiding relationship has taught me a permanent Joy. I wish everyone could hear and understand the truth presented in Jessica's Sonship books, for they would change their lives like they did mine. In three short months, this young woman has taught me more about my relationship with Jesus than I learned in 15 years of prison. Thank you Jessica for following the unction of the Holy Spirit and allowing Him to be the Voice of Truth in my life.

--Daniel Barnes

INTRODUCTION

This is the fourth and final book of The Sonship Series. While there are an infinite number of things we could discuss, this is the final piece that was on my heart to write for this series. My hope was to lay the groundwork for people to be able to launch into a deeper relationship with Yahweh, Jesus, and Holy Spirit. From that relationship, we have everything we could ever need or possibly want to know! So if you have a connection to Jesus, you have everything you need!

In the previous books, we explored the beliefs and perspectives of sonship as well as soul healing and health. Up till now, this series has focused inward on our own processes and relationship with Jesus. Our past, fears, soul blocks, and wounds all throttle the good things that God has in store for us. Once we have addressed our past, we can access our inheritance. As we renew our mind, we can walk in authority and power while we take back the earth (and other realms) for Jesus! There is an infinite frontier for the sons of God. It's a wonderful adventure where we get to love and be loved by Yahweh throughout the realms, ages, and dimensions!

It is important that we cultivate our own momentum and sustainability as we explore our authority. Revivals and movements can be great and launch people forward. (It was a revival in my youth group that woke me up and completely changed my life!) BUT too often, believers only ride the waves of movements. They never learn how to cultivate their own authority and their own walk with Yahweh. In this book, I hope to give you the understanding and foundation needed to be able to create and maintain your own momentum in Christ SO THAT you can stand firm and walk in the unique expression of God on the earth that you already are! I believe there are intense times ahead, but I also believe that the sons of God who don't harden their hearts will be like radiant lights in the midst of the darkness. I want to help prepare the sons of God for hard times because these truly are the most exciting times to be alive. We CAN walk in abundant life and even joy in the midst of suffering and difficulty, and I am convinced that we will see the greatest outpouring of the Spirit of God that the world has ever seen.

To be honest, I was hesitant to write this last book because many believers idolize moving in power and miracles. I want to be very clear that JESUS is THE prize. The gospel is the good news of our redemption and reconciliation into the family of God! The power and miracles come as a byproduct of our relationship with Yahweh, but believers often short-change themselves by making an idol of miracles, power, and what they can get from God. The power, glory, and miracles are nothing compared to Yahweh Himself. I want to say that again...the power, glory, and miracles are NOTHING compared to Yahweh Himself. I hope this series has helped you fall in love with Yahweh for HIM. And I hope this final book helps strengthen your relationship with Him as we explore some of the mysteries of God's authority and power.

Chapter One

FIRST, WE RECEIVE

I recently went on a trip to Moravian Falls. It had been a childhood desire of mine to visit that spiritual place, and I was so excited that the time had finally come! I had been told stories of incredible encounters, and I was expectant and eager for a similar experience. My friend and I arrived at the falls and excitedly got settled into our cabin. The atmosphere was spiritually charged with angels, but for some reason, it fell short of my expectations, and I found myself disappointed. I brushed off the disappointment and focused on my excitement for the next day's trip to Prayer Mountain. Early the next morning, we arrived at Prayer Mountain, hopeful and excited to see what Jesus had for us. After exploring the mountain and finding the perfect spot, I sat down to engage with Yahweh. Again, after all the hype, I found myself disappointed on Prayer Mountain. I brought my disappointment to Yahweh. First, His peace and goodness comforted my heart, then He dropped the revelation bomb, "The times when you have been seeking a power encounter from a person or event have been letdowns to you in recent years because you already have the very thing within you that you are seeking. It's better for you to not have a visitation... because then you will continue to look to a place or others to be refreshed." Yahweh paused for effect, then continued, "All of the prophetic words you have received recently and every angelic visitation has fallen short because external encounters don't come close to the internal reality and glory you already have. It is better for me to NOT give you a visitation because then I would be feeding the desire to look outward instead of inward." And in a moment, all my disappointment regarding the trip vanished. My heart shifted immediately, and I enjoyed the rest of our stay in contentment and peace because what

I already carried within me was WAY more powerful than any encounter I could have, even at Moravian Falls.

Jesus told me years ago, "You don't need a visitation because you have a habitation of my Presence." It stuck with me like glue, but my desire to visit Moravian Falls predated that revelation. That childhood desire had not been sifted by my current revelation and maturity. I knew to some level that visitations fell short of what I already carried, but what Yahweh said took me one layer deeper. It was a deeper revealing of not looking out but looking within. I don't need to visit spiritually charged places...I AM a spiritually charged place. I don't need to look for portals... I AM a portal.

As I marinated in what Yahweh had just told me, Jesus began explaining the importance of having every area of my heart surrendered to (in agreement with) Truth. He further showed me that there was NOTHING I could DO to get there. My healing and breakthrough were a gift that I could simply RECEIVE. The revelation came to me in poem form...

Finished

I ascend the Heavens to meet with Yahweh
There I find I'm already with Him

So I bring my past to lay before Him
He tells me He's already forgotten it

Then I bring my soul pain for Him to heal
And I see that He's already healed it

What else is there?
What more needs to be done?

He prepares the table before me
He fills my cup to overflowing
He restores my soul

It truly was finished

There's nothing I can do but receive

Receive His love that's already there

Receive His healing that's already done

Receive my place that's already given

There's nothing I can do but receive

As I receive, there's a door

A door to more

Once I receive

I can rule and reign

But not before

Because then I'll think it's me

There's nothing I can do

Yet nothing I can't do

Before I receive, there's every limit

As I receive, there is no limit

Jesus finished it in me

And now I will finish it on the earth

This poem reveals how to walk in sonship and authority. Many believers try to DO before they know how to BE a son. As this poem unfolded, I understood clearly that we can only RECEIVE everything that we need. We can't DO anything for our salvation, healing, or provision. Yahweh prepares the table. HE fills our cup to overflowing. Jesus provided everything we needed for life and godliness. HE finished it. All we can possibly do is receive. Receive our salvation that was already provided. Receive our healing that was already paid for. Receive our place and inheritance that was already given. We can't DO anything for ourselves. It is a GIFT.

Once our heart receives this gift, it is from that place that we can DO things out of the abundance in our hearts. If we try to DO before we learn how to BE, everything we do will fall short (and even bring death) because our actions are done from the Tree of Knowledge. People (and religion) focus on our actions, but Yahweh looks at the heart. He sees the brokenness, pain, and dysfunction that we live in when we operate from the Tree of Knowledge. What's worse is that we are blind to most of the brokenness, pain, and dysfunction...because it's all we have known.

In Chapter 4 of Book 2 (*Growing in Sonship*), I discussed the Tree of Knowledge and the Tree of Life. Summed up, we are all born into the Tree of Knowledge (the tangible manifestation of our ability to reject God), and until we learn how to live from the Tree of Life (the tangible manifestation of choosing God's abundant life), we will be stuck in a perpetual cycle of dysfunction because we are living from the wrong tree. The key to learning how to live from the Tree of Life is the renewing of our mind. As we surrender every area of our heart to Jesus and agree with His truth, we become more refined, healed, and made new until we have been wholly transformed.

So far in the Sonship Series, I have only taught on how to BE a son. I didn't want to teach how to walk in power and authority before believers learned how to RECEIVE what Jesus has for us. We can't walk in the fullness of abundant life while using the Tree of Knowledge. But when we live from the Tree of Life, everything we do brings life. We are life-giving spirits, but if we don't know our identity, we will be stuck in our dysfunction and brokenness. Our perspective/beliefs on our identity, life, and God affects EVERY area of our life. We do not see things as they truly are. We see things as WE are. What our soul perceives about life is what our soul believes... even if it's not true. Perceived is believed. We all live in our own self-created perception of reality. This is why soul transformation is SO important. As we RECEIVE truth, we are transformed. It's a beautiful transformation to wake up from our perception of the world and learn to see, love, and live from Yahweh's perspective. From THAT place, we can more effectively walk in God's power and authority because we are living from the Tree of Life. Until our soul is in agreement with the tree of life (renewed by truth), we will only be able to walk in measures of authority because our soul is still wrestling with truth.

Spiritual authority is wielding God's power through the empowerment of Holy Spirit. It is our inheritance as sons of God. This means we do not have to strive to walk in authority. It is a GIFT. Many believers are trying to wield God's power and walk in spiritual authority BEFORE their souls have been transformed by Yahweh. Our souls do not have to be fully healed to walk in a measure of spiritual authority. BUT...the more unrenewed mind our mind is, the more we will be internally resisting the very power we are trying to wield. The more we wrestle with the truth, the more our soul will also wrestle with being in agreement with God's power. Remember that to preserve our free will, God gives our souls the choice to choose Jesus and receive this gift, OR we can choose to believe lies and reject all the benefits that Jesus has given us.

Let's look at the disciples when they were given authority by Jesus...

> Luke 9:1 (ESV) "And he called the twelve together and gave them power and authority over all demons and to cure diseases,"

Then, at least once when the disciples were sent out, they weren't able to kick the demons out. They were given authority but couldn't wield it...

> Matthew 17:19 (BSB) "Afterward the disciples came to Jesus privately and asked, 'Why couldn't we drive it out?' 'Because you have so little faith,' He answered. 'For truly I tell you, if you have faith the size of a mustard seed, you can say to this mountain, "Move from here to there," and it will move. Nothing will be impossible for you.'"

The disciples had the authority, but in this case, they weren't able to wield it in the areas where their minds were not renewed. In the Bible, we see that the disciples did other miracles, but when facing this demoniac, their faith was shaken. The same thing happens in our soul. Areas where we lack faith expose places in our soul that are agreeing with lies of the enemy. Any part of our soul that has not been transformed by truth will operate from an unsound mind. This unsoundness throttles our ability to walk in God's power. Spiritual authority is our inheritance, but it is one that we grow into. It is part of our process of BEcoming, and we go at the pace of our soul's readiness and willingness to submit to truth and be transformed.

We have the choice to operate in an earthly/soulish way or in Yahweh's/Heaven's way. Obviously, our goal as sons is to operate and live like Jesus did, but we currently are still in the process of becoming like Jesus. We create dissonance within our soul when we are trying to walk in the power of God but are still living from dysfunction in our soul. The soulish parts of our heart reject the things of God. Plainly put, we are unyielding (not submitting) to the very power we are trying to walk in.

> John 6:29 (TPT) "Jesus answered, '_The work you can do for God starts with believing in the One he has sent._'" [Emphasis mine]

The more we believe Jesus (agree with truth in our soul), the more power and authority we will walk in. First, we receive. Then, we can do. Please understand, I am not suggesting that we wait until we are "ready" before we go and start walking in authority. It's not about us being "ready." We learn as we walk it out. A baby learns by watching the parents and walking it out for itself. In the same way, we learn as we go AND practice. Sometimes we can be unaware that there is a part of our soul that is unrenewed UNTIL it is exposed.

You can read the manual on how to drive a car, but you will still be an inexperienced driver until you actually get behind the wheel and practice. Yahweh is not looking for people who are "ready" enough. He is just waiting for our "YES" because, with that, anything is possible. Remember that everything the Father does is relational. It's about doing things together WITH Him.

Walking in authority is just one more facet of our journey with Yahweh. We are SONS of a GOOD Father. He will father our hearts and actions as we grow in Him. Walking in authority is no different. We are HIS kids, given HIS Spirit, and walking in HIS authority! HE is faithful to us and invested in us. He is a good father who takes on the responsibility of teaching us how to walk in His power. He even goes so far as to clean up our messes by bringing GOOD from everything we do. The extent of His goodness knows no end!

Before we go any further, I do want to mention that spiritual power is NOT a direct sign of intimacy or maturity. It is possible for someone to operate in the gifts of the Holy Spirit with an unrenewed soul. However, when people's actions are rooted in the Tree of Knowledge, the fruit of their actions leads people to be hurt, confused, and disheartened towards God. We can move in the gifts of the Spirit from the Tree of Knowledge (which is what religion is), or we can move in the power and authority of Yahweh from the Tree of Life (which is what this book is about). Now that we have cleared that up, let's explore how to cultivate authority!

Chapter Two

WHOSE AUTHORITY?

I wanted to start this chapter by discussing WHOSE authority we have. But then I realized, *"HOW can I possibly describe the all-encompassing authority that God has? I have a pea-brained understanding, and I know that words won't even come close to beginning to describe His authority!"* There is none like Him. The Uncreated One. The Alpha and Omega. The author and finisher. God IS the definition of authority. Every power, force, and energy in this life was created by Him, for Him, and are held together by Him. Nothing can exist apart from Him. I want to be VERY clear...my MINISCULE understanding of Yahweh and His authority doesn't even scratch the surface of His vastness. But I will share what little I know, in words that will fall short, in hopes of bringing a little more understanding about God's authority into your journey of sonship. Let's start in John...

> *John 1:1-5 (TPT) "In the beginning the Living Expression was already there. And the Living Expression was with God, yet fully God. They were together—face-to-face, in the very beginning. And through his creative inspiration this Living Expression made all things, for nothing has existence apart from him! A fountain of life was in him, for his life is light for all humanity. And this Light never fails to shine through the darkness— Light that darkness could not overcome!"*

For us to walk in HIS authority, it helps to take a good long look at the NATURE of Yahweh. After all, His nature is what we are growing into! What does He do, and when does He do it? What examples did Jesus give us when He was on earth? Many things will probably make you uncomfortable. There are still many questions about what God did that leave ME perplexed!

For this chapter, I list some of what God (Father, Son, and Holy Spirit) says about Himself and His actions, but please know that there is MUCH more to explore than this list. I provided the lists to help jumpstart your exploration...but there is infinitely more to discover about God! Remember that as soon as we think we know something, we stop growing in that area. Stay humble and stay hungry! Now, let's take a look at how God describes Himself...

YAHWEH'S "I AM" STATEMENTS FOUND IN THE BIBLE:

- I am slow to anger and filled with unfailing love (Exodus 34:6)
- I am that I am (Exodus 3:14)
- I am with you, and I am your God (Isaiah 41:10)
- I am the maker of all things (Isaiah 44:24)
- I am the Lord (Isaiah 45:18 and many more places)
- I am the Alpha and the Omega (Revelation 1:8)

JESUS' "I AM" STATEMENTS FOUND IN THE BIBLE:

(Remember, He is the EXACT reflection of the Father)

- I am the bread of life (John 6:35)
- I am the light of the world (John 8:12)
- I am the way, the truth, and the life (John 14:6)
- I am the door (John 10:9)
- I am the good shepherd (John 10:11)
- I am the resurrection and the life (John 11:25-26)
- I am the vine (John 15:5)
- I am the son of God (Matthew 27:43)

I suggest taking time to meditate on each of these "I am" statements that God says about Himself. The statements that Yahweh makes about Himself show us a picture of who He is and what the authority we have been given looks like. And most of the statements that Jesus says about Himself, He also says we are, so pay close attention to them! For example, WE are the light of the world. WE are kings and priests. WE are sons of God. While there are many things Jesus said that apply to us, we will never be JESUS Himself (the savior, creator, or healer of the world). We are sons of God and one spirit with Jesus which means we will take on characteristics of Jesus (*like being the light of the world*) without actually being Him. So, the more we study the "I Am" statements of God, the more we will understand what the authority we are given looks like AND grow in our identity.

After meditating on what God says about Himself, it helps to then study His actions and explore when and how God did the things we read about in the Bible. What God says and does in scripture are examples of His power and use of authority. BUT as we study scripture, remember that religion has twisted our perception and interpretation of the Bible. This means it is vitally important to ASK God about what we see recorded in scripture. There is so much mystery and misunderstanding around His actions in the Bible that it is easy to miss the beauty and goodness in the stories we read. As you explore God's actions in the Bible, I suggest you ask Jesus to show you the heart of the Father in each one...

SOME OF WHAT WE SAW YAHWEH DO IN THE BIBLE:
(*Not in order*)

- Created everything
- Banned Adam and Eve from the garden
- Scrambled everyone's languages
- Took Enoch straight to Heaven
- Destroyed the whole earth in a flood
- Destroyed Sodom and Gomorrah and turned Lot's wife into salt.
- Made a one-sided covenant with Abraham (Yahweh did all the work)
- Wrestled with Jacob

- Spoke to Moses through a burning bush
- Brought Israel out of Egypt, sent plagues to Egypt, hardened Pharaoh's heart, split the Red Sea
- Made a covenant with Israel
- Led Israelites through the desert with a pillar of fire/cloud, revealed Himself at Mt Sinai, sent manna and quail, had a rock (Jesus) filled with water follow them, sent serpents to kill grumbling Israelites, forbid Moses to enter the Promised Land after one act of disobedience
- Provided a land flowing with milk and honey, then provided kings at the Israelites' request
- Sent calamity, famine, droughts, and allowed war and enslavement to come to the Israelites...and then delivered Israel many times
- Laughs at all who oppose Him
- Took Elijah up in a pillar of fire
- Fought the battle for Jehoshaphat while the army worshipped
- Saved Shadrack, Meshack, and Abednego from the furnace
- Shut the lions' mouths

SOME OF WHAT WE SAW JESUS DO IN THE BIBLE:

(Not in order)

- Turned water into wine
- Healed the sick
- Raised the dead
- Cleansed lepers
- Cast out demons
- Calmed the storm
- Cursed the fig tree
- Multiplied food
- Offended the religious
- Flipped tables and used a whip

- Forgave sinners
- Called disciples that were...average
- Took naps
- Walked away from the crowd to pray
- Didn't answer every question (Matthew 21:27)
- Walked on water
- Washed his disciples' feet
- Walked through walls
- Disappeared in front of crowds
- Translocated (also known as teleported)
- Laid His life down for us
- Came back to life and then ascended

SOME OF WHAT WE SAW HOLY SPIRIT DO IN THE BIBLE:
(Not in order)

- Hovered over the waters at creation
- Descended like a dove over Jesus
- Struck Ananias and Sapphira dead when they lied
- Baptized the disciples in Acts and manifested as flames of fire

In the Bible, we see many great stories that align with who God says He is *(like saving Israel over and over or sending His Son to die for us!)*. In the midst of all the obviously good things we see God do, there are also lots of puzzling stories about God in the Bible. Some of the most bizarre instances are the actions that seem contrary to His "I am" statements (like hardening people's hearts). What God says and does often goes beyond our pea-brain's ability to understand. Regardless of our understanding of God's actions, it is important to remember that He ALWAYS does good things, even if we don't see it that way...

> *Isaiah 45:7 (BSB) "I form the light and create the*

darkness; I bring prosperity and create calamity. I,
the LORD, do all these things."

This is an odd verse...and a very unsettling one for those who are not confident in the goodness of God. But remember that every verse is an invitation to grow our relationship with Yahweh. Our perception and "knowledge" of God affects HOW we read this verse! For those not anchored in the goodness of God, this verse validates all the questions and concerns our flesh has regarding the concept of God. For those who are confident in Yahweh, this verse does not bother us because we do not fear adversity or hard times. We live at peace and with an <u>unshakable confidence</u> in the goodness of God. We KNOW that GOODNESS is woven into <u>everything</u> we do. We can't lose. Yahweh is our strength. He is GOOD, and everything He does is rooted in love. If adversity does come, it will work out for GOOD...there is nothing to fear...ever! Abundant LIFE is the only option, and the more we grow, the more we will see the goodness of God in everything He does.

> *Psalms 119:68 (NLT) "You are good and do only*
> *good; teach me your decrees."*

Most people shut down or ignore spiritual things outside their box. BUT there is invitation and revelation hidden within the mystery IF we don't harden our hearts. As our soul softens to things outside our box, little by little Holy Spirit unveils more of the mysteries previously hidden for us. In all of the mystery, the bottom line is that God is GOOD, and everything He does is good. Over time and through relationship with God, we will grow to understand His ways...falling more in love with Him as the mysteries reveal more of His kindness and glory.

To grow in sonship and walk in His authority, I feel like it is important for us to explore and embrace ALL of who God is. We will have a biased view of God if we only embrace the parts of God we think we understand and are comfortable with. I don't want to get to know just one attribute of Yahweh and block out the fullness of who He is. Below is a poem I wrote when I was confronted with the mysteries of God being beyond my boxes and ideas.

Color Outside the Lines

Take me to the edge of myself
I want to be undone

Make me uncomfortable
I want to know Your heart
Captivate and overwhelm me
I just want You

Break up the ground
Tear down the walls
I'm ready for the mess
I want it all

Unthrottled, unbridled
Out of the box

Color outside the lines
Color on me
Color on You
Color outside the lines

If we want to be like God, we have to embrace ALL of who He is. Currently, we have a pea-brain understanding of what that means and looks like, but our heart can still say YES to all of Him regardless of our understanding. Will you choose Him even if He offends you? Will you still choose Him even if you don't understand Him? In the midst of the mysteries of God's word, I have learned to trust Yahweh and keep an open mind toward what He does and says...even when it makes me uncomfortable or is outside of my box.

Even though there is much I don't understand, there are many things I am CONFIDENT in. I know He is GOOD, very GOOD.

I know He IS the definition of love. I know He not only is my Creator, but He is also my Healer and Redeemer. He has taken away my pain and given me abundant life. He has empowered me with HIS Spirit and chosen to bind Himself to me for all eternity when all I did was fail and fall short. I have seen God transform my greatest weaknesses into my greatest strengths. He has given me joy for my mourning. No one can talk me out of these things.

There are still many Bible stories that I am puzzled about. For example, God has only just begun to unveil understanding about His wrath and judgment. It is easy for our pea-brains to become stuck on the things we don't understand. Many people become frustrated and even lose their faith when they perceive "inconsistencies" in the scriptures. I want to challenge you to embrace God in the midst of not understanding. God is already outside of your box and understanding...it is just a matter of us accepting that reality!

Instead of rejecting the things I don't understand, I created an "I don't know" metaphorical shelf that I set things on regularly. Significant dreams that I don't understand are set on this shelf. Verses, Bible stories, and testimonies that fluster my soul are also set on this shelf. Instead of creating a theology around something I don't understand (or instead of rejecting it altogether), I hold these things to ponder in my heart until Jesus speaks to me about them. Jesus knows my heart, so He knows that I want revelation for the things I set on my "I don't know" shelf. As my soul grows in maturity and capacity to trust, Jesus will take things off the shelf to enlighten me on them. In my experience, Jesus doesn't speak to me about things until I am ready to hear and receive the truth. So much of the timing of the Lord comes down to our soul's process. Having patience is KEY to growing in sonship and authority because there are lots of mysteries surrounding God that we don't understand yet.

For example, I was bothered that Yahweh did not warn the other families in Bethlehem to get up and flee before the soldiers came to kill the babies. What the scriptures show is that Joseph had a dream and fled before Herod gave the command to kill the children under two years old. Knowing that God cared about ALL of His children, I set my curiosity on the "I don't know" shelf. I don't know how long I pondered that thought, but one day Jesus answered me. He told me, "ALL of the families were warned, but only one listened to my voice. Joseph and Mary recognized my voice AND acted on it." Instantly my heart was at peace again. He DID warn them, but they chose not to listen to (or they heard but didn't act) what God said.

Let's take God's wrath as another example. The concept of God's wrath is filtered through our HUMAN understanding of anger. There is no other way for us to process Yahweh's pure and just wrath when all we have ever known are HUMAN examples. When studying the word "wrath" in the scriptures, the original Hebrew word can mean "His face is turned towards." "His face is turned towards Adam" vs "God's wrath was towards Adam" have two TOTALLY different meanings! Sometimes the word "wrath" in our Bible actually meant "grieved or filled with sorrow" in the original Hebrew text. Then there are other times when "wrath" in the Hebrew does actually mean wrath or very angry. But even when God IS angry, we also know from scripture that God's anger is very different from human anger (James 1:20).

So, when studying any part of God's character, it is important to read the scripture WITH Holy Spirit so HE can teach us in all things. Interpreting God through our human filters will ALWAYS miss the mark terribly. God's pure and just wrath is a mystery to our human pea-brains UNTIL our soul is renewed and transformed to the point that we have the capacity to receive the revelation and mystery of His wrath.

Most believers focus on one or two attributes of God, like His love or His judgment. Then they build their theology, ministry, and life around that attribute (or attributes) that they focused on. But when we only focus on one or two of His attributes, then we are blinding ourselves to the fullness of God that is available to us. Yahweh will never fit into the tidy little boxes that we make for Him. This also means that what it looks like for us to be like Him and walk in His authority will look very different than what we expect.

> *1 Corinthians 13:12 (TPT)* "*For now we see but a faint reflection of riddles and mysteries as though reflected in a mirror, but one day we will see face-to-face. My understanding is incomplete now, but one day I will understand everything, just as everything about me has been fully understood.*"

> *1 Thessalonians 1:5a (TPT)* "*For our gospel came to you not merely in the form of words but in the mighty power infused with the Holy Spirit and deep conviction...*"

Faith is the foundation of our relationship with God...regardless of our pea-brained understanding of Him. In the midst of so much mystery, we can still stand firm on what God tells us. Yahweh calls us HIS child and tells us that HE fills our cup. HE prepares the table. HE fights for us. HE restores our soul. He is good beyond measure, and He is more invested in our growth than anyone else. And for some odd reason, the only thing we have to do is receive what HE has already done...

> *John 6:28-29 (NLT)* "*They replied, "We want to perform God's works, too. What should we do?" Jesus told them, "This is the only work God wants from you: Believe in the one he has sent."* [Emphasis mine]

Is there mystery surrounding God? Yes. Can we choose Him in the midst of the unknown? Yes. We were created for oneness, and oneness goes beyond our understanding. All we are asked to do is believe (choose Him). With our "YES" to Jesus, everything else falls into place.

The more I embrace who He is, the more I will be like Him.

The more I trust Him, the more I can walk in His authority.

The more I understand Him, the more I can wield His power.

Chapter Three

HOW MUCH POWER DOES OUR ENEMY HAVE?

Much more can be gained from focusing on the Father than we could ever gain from learning about our enemy. This being said, I do want to take time to explain the enemy's authority and power because we interact with our enemy constantly (knowingly and unknowingly). God and the Heavenly hosts have power, the enemy has power, and we have power. So it is helpful to discuss the boundaries and power our enemy has so we don't become dismayed or surrender territory to them.

> *Ephesians 6:12 (NLT) "For we are not fighting against flesh-and-blood enemies, but against evil rulers and authorities of the unseen world, against mighty powers in this dark world, and against evil spirits in the heavenly places."*

The story of our enemy begins before the earth was made. Lucifer thought he could become like Yahweh. His wisdom became corrupted (Ezekiel 28:17), and God cast him out of Heaven. Lucifer is then referred to as "Satan" in the Bible, which simply means *adversary*. Because of Revelation 12:4, it is speculated that about 1/3 of the angels joined the corruption and fell with Satan. Our enemy has many names, faces, and positions, such as demons, fallen angels, princes, powers, and evil spirits. Regardless of their titles, this adversary of ours hates us, is jealous of us, and wants to steal, kill, and destroy our lives. Our enemy can never be trusted...even when what they say *feels* true to our broken and hurting soul. Every word they speak brings death regardless of the facts they twist into their temptations.

When the world was created, the authority to rule and reign over the earth was given to Adam and Eve. They were called to SUBDUE the earth and transform it to look like Heaven Instead, Adam and Eve allowed themselves to be subdued by the serpent. They chose to believe the serpent's lies said over what Yahweh said. When they ate of the Tree of Knowledge, their actions released death over the whole earth. Satan grew in his authority and power by usurping Adam and Eve's authority. He became the "prince of this world" (John 12:31), the "ruler of the authority of the air" (Ephesians 2:2), and the "god of this world" (2 Corinthians 4:4).

> *1 John 5:19 (AMP) "We know [for a fact] that we are of God, and the whole world [around us] lies in the power of the evil one [opposing God and His precepts]."*

After the fall, all of creation was subdued under the curse of sin. We were powerless to get ourselves out of the mess we put ourselves in. We fell short, and no amount of following the law or doing good could heal our broken souls! We once were under the power of the enemy, but we have been set FREE through Jesus.

> *Colossians 1:13 (TPT) "He has rescued us completely from the tyrannical rule of darkness and has translated us into the kingdom realm of his beloved Son."*

> *Colossians 2:15 (NLT) "In this way, he disarmed the spiritual rulers and authorities. He shamed them publicly by his victory over them on the cross."*

Just setting us free from sin was not enough. We had to be

EMPOWERED again, and Jesus did just that. We were given His Spirit and seated in Heavenly places. Jesus did far above what we could ask or imagine. We didn't earn or deserve any of it, but everything and MORE was given back to us through Jesus.

> 1 John 4:4 (NLT) "But you belong to God, my dear children. You have already won a victory over those people, because the Spirit who lives in you is greater than the spirit who lives in the world." [Emphasis mine]

> 2 Peter 1:3 (NLT) "By his divine power, God has given us everything we need for living a godly life. We have received all of this by coming to know him, the one who called us to himself by means of his marvelous glory and excellence."

So the enemy didn't have power, then we gave them our power, then Jesus came and took back the keys and disarmed our enemy. Why then do we still see SO much evil happening on the earth? As long as there is free will to not choose Yahweh, there will always be a way for the enemy to influence the earth. Our ignorance is their power.

> Ephesians 4:27 (ESV) "and give no opportunity to the devil."

We ignorantly believe the enemy's lies and empower them in our lives...and worse, we empower the enemy on the earth. Spiritual beings don't have a physical body, so our enemy is continually looking for a bridge from the spirit realm to earth. Our adversary is bound to the spiritual realm...until people get involved and become a bridge. When our actions stem from the lies we are believing, we become the hands and feet of the enemy on the earth.

> 1 Peter 5:8 (BSB) "Be sober-minded and alert. Your adversary the devil prowls around like a roaring lion, seeking someone to devour."

They roam the earth seeking whom they may devour. The key word there is SEEKING. They are seeking whom they may devour...because they don't have the power or authority to kill as they please. Much of the authority the enemy operates in is given to them by us. WE empower the enemy any time we agree with their lies. Whatever we focus on (spend time or emotion on), we give life and energy to. If the enemy can affect our emotions, they become empowered by us. For example, we feed (give life to) unforgiveness when we harbor bitterness against someone. The enemy is roaming the earth, looking for a way to gain power and authority on the earth. Adam and Eve were the first to give the enemy power on the earth, but we do the same thing every day when we agree with lies and empower the enemy in our life.

Here me clearly, our enemy is NOT as powerful as people think and fear. Someone may *believe* that the enemy has a lot of authority or that "the devil made me do it", but our enemy is not that powerful. The devil can't MAKE us do anything. GOD gave us our free will, and the enemy is not allowed to take that from us...ever. If the enemy was as powerful as people think he is and had the ability to remove our free will...then we would all be dead (because that's what he ultimately wants!). Basically, our enemy is a master manipulator.

> John 14:30-31a (NLT) "I don't have much more time to talk to you, because the ruler of this world approaches. He has no power over me, but I will do what the Father requires of me..." [Emphasis mine]

Remember that we are ONE with Jesus. If Satan had no power over Jesus, then he has no power over us! Our enemy can tempt us, and attempt to influence or deceive us, but the blinding and binding is our own doing through our agreement with them. The more we agree with the lies, the more we are swayed or influenced by the enemy's deception. But it is always and only an influence that they have over us. Once someone decides they are done playing the enemy's game, the enemy has lost. No one can truly "sell their soul to the devil" and be beyond God's reach.

> *Romans 8:38-39 (NLT) "And I am convinced that nothing can ever separate us from God's love. Neither death nor life, neither angels nor demons, neither our fears for today nor our worries about tomorrow—not even the powers of hell can separate us from God's love. No power in the sky above or in the earth below—indeed, nothing in all of creation will ever be able to separate us from the love of God that is revealed in Christ Jesus our Lord."*

As I mentioned earlier, our enemy became the "prince of this world," the "ruler of the authority of the air," and the "god of this world" after the fall. Jesus DID disarm our enemy, but creation is still subdued under the curse of sin. Creation and the "air" (atmosphere) are still under the influence of our adversary. That is why creation is groaning for us, the sons of God, to be revealed.

> *Romans 8:19-21 (BSB) "The creation waits in eager expectation for the revelation of the sons of God. For the creation was subjected to futility, not by its own will, but because of the One who subjected it, in hope that the creation itself will be set free from its bondage to decay and brought into the glorious freedom of the children of God."*

Now there are unique circumstances when the enemy is allowed a greater measure of power over the earth, but these times are exceptions. For example, God gave Satan permission to afflict Job. (More detail about Job coming later on in this book!) We also know that Satan asked to sift Peter like wheat. Then there are multiple times mentioned in Revelation when different parties (beast, dragon, locusts, etc.) will have the authority to wreak havoc on the earth during the transition of the ages. While we may be tempted to, it is best to not build a theology around isolated events that we don't fully understand. Similar to Paul's thorn in his side, there are a handful of SPECIAL circumstances in the Bible that are exceptions.

The Bible lays out some clear boundaries that our adversary must abide by...

- God will not allow us to be tempted more than we can stand [1 Corinthians 10:13]
- We can do all things through Christ [Philippians 4:13]
- Sin does not have dominion over us [Romans 6:14]
- We are free from the law of sin and death. Nothing can separate us from the love of God [Romans 8:1-39]
- We WILL face trials, but Jesus has overcome [John 16:33]
- Jesus disarmed the spiritual rulers and authorities [Colossians 2:15]
- With the armor of God, we can stand against the schemes of the enemy [Ephesians 6:11]
- If we use the shield of faith, we can stop every flaming arrow from the enemy [Ephesians 6:16]
- Submitted to God, we can resist the devil, and he will flee [James 4:7]

Furthermore, God promises to work ALL things out for GOOD for those that love God (Romans 8:28). This is all VERY good news for us! There are boundaries and limits put on our adversary, but even in the times when the enemy lands a punch...God still works it out for OUR good! We can't lose. It is incredible! We really did get the best deal in the universe. So yes, our enemy is here with some power, and sometimes they will have more power than other times. But even then, their attempts against us still work out for our good. Every time the enemy attacks, they risk making us stronger instead of tearing us down as they hope. The cool thing about sifting is that sifting HIGHLIGHTS the impurities! Every time we get angry, offended, fearful, or agree with any other lie, it brings to light an area of our heart that we can renew and get healed! Every sifting brings the opportunity for more breakthrough!

It really changes everything when we understand how little power our enemy has over us. If we don't believe any of their lies and deception, they have NO hold on us. And IF we find an area that they do have a hold in... all we have to do is bring that part of our heart to Jesus so it can be healed and restored!

> John 1:5 (NLT) "The light shines in the darkness, and the darkness can never extinguish it." [Emphasis mine]

> 1 John 4:4 (NLT) "But you belong to God, my dear children. You have already won a victory over those people, because the Spirit who lives in you is greater than the spirit who lives in the world." [Emphasis mine]

So we either win, or God redeems a situation...and we still win! So what makes the difference between our two options? The quick answer is us...WE make the difference. God (obviously) knows what's up...even the enemy knows what's up. The big question is, what are WE going to decide to do/who are we going to believe? Our enemy has some power, but not over us...

> 1 John 5:18-19 (NLT) "We know that God's children do not make a practice of sinning, for God's Son holds them securely, and the evil one cannot touch them. We know that we are children of God and that the world around us is under the control of the evil one." [Emphasis mine]

> James 4:7 (ESV) "Submit yourselves therefore to God. Resist the devil, and he will flee from you." [Emphasis mine]

So our enemy has power over the earth, but not over us. The enemy has no power over Jesus, so the enemy has no power over us...unless WE empower the enemy by agreeing with their lies. "Submit yourselves to God" was written to believers, which shows us that we can be a believer and not be submitted to God. Agreeing with lies is the same thing as submitting to the enemy. Unknowingly, we are delegating our authority to the enemy...just like Adam and Eve did. No one would knowingly agree with the lies of our enemy who wants to steal, kill, and destroy our lives! But when we are not confident in Yahweh, we will continually take the bait of the enemy and agree with their lies instead of standing firm on Yahweh and His truth.

In reality, the enemy's authority over us is actually gifted to them...by us! They don't have any legal grounds to keep the power over us that they are holding. So the moment we wake up to the reality of the lies, we can take BACK our authority, and there's NOTHING the enemy can do about it. Victory is ours the moment we choose Jesus. He's already GIVEN us victory. It is finished! When we receive His words and victory, then our soul awakens to that reality.

Even though victory is our reality, it is not usually received instantly in our soul. Pain and soul wounds usually take up a large portion of our soul's thinking/feeling capacity. Dealing with the enemy usually *feels* overwhelming and foreboding, but we *feel* that way only because our soul is believing lies and operating from wounds. As we renew our mind, we transform those broken areas of our soul. This then lessens the weight and influence the pain and soul wounds hold over us.

All that the enemy has over us is the lies that we are agreeing with. Once we don't bite, their game is over. Because of our oneness with Jesus, we can be free from the enemy's influence once we decide to be. It usually takes time to untwist our soul from the entanglement of lies, BUT we don't do it alone. This IS the journey of SONship...we walk WITH Jesus in everything. Through our friendship with Jesus, He will teach us how to address the lies we believe in our soul and how to address the enemy in the world around us.

In BEcoming Whole (Book 3), we discussed in depth how to address soul wounds and lies. When we deal with our enemy, it is a very similar process. Everything in our life comes back to ABIDING and INTIMACY with Jesus. Through our relationship with Him, HE shows us what to do with each adversary we face. There is not one answer or formula for how to do things in the spirit. Sometimes Jesus silenced demons. Sometimes He commanded them. Sometimes He ignored them. Sometimes He went to physical places to address demonic strongholds in the natural. We also see in the Old Testament that Yahweh gave different instructions to the Israelites to defeat their enemies. Some great examples: Joshua was told to walk around the wall of Jericho and shout. Gideon was instructed to cover lamps with pots. Jehoshaphat was told to simply stand in the field and worship. NONE of those things should have defeated their enemies, but they did!

The point of this life is to walk WITH God through a personal relationship. There is no formula for "how to address the enemy." This life is about growing as sons and learning how to walk with the Father as Jesus did. Through abiding, Yahweh WILL teach us how to defeat our enemies. He WANTS us to be victorious! God's desire for us is to grow to be strong and mature sons. We saw an example of this when the Israelites went into the Promised Land. It says in Judges that God LEFT giants in the land FOR the Israelites to grow.

> Judges 3:1 (NLT) "These are the nations that the LORD left in the land to test those Israelites who had not experienced the wars of Canaan."

God is focused on our heart and our growth because He knows what happens in our lives as we mature. Amazingly, conquering giants is NOURISHMENT for our soul.

> Numbers 14:9 (BSB) "Only do not rebel against the LORD, and do not be afraid of the people of the land, for they will be like bread for us. Their protection has been removed, and the LORD is with us. Do not be afraid of them!" [Emphasis mine]

Suddenly our enemy doesn't seem so threatening once we view

him as bread for our soul and a catalyst for our breakthrough.

> *Genesis 50:20 (NLT) "You intended to harm me, but God intended it all for good. He brought me to this position so I could save the lives of many people."*

> *Romans 8:28 (NLT) "And we know that God causes everything to work together for the good of those who love God and are called according to his purpose for them."*

> *Romans 8:31 (NLT) "What shall we say about such wonderful things as these? If God is for us, who can ever be against us?"*

We can't lose. VICTORY is our reality and identity. It is a humble victory because Jesus did the work, but we are triumphant nonetheless. Yahweh redeems every attack of the enemy to make the situation BETTER than it was before the attack! We might not see the results on earth in our lifetime, but this earth is just a vapor. From Heaven's perspective, VICTORY has already been finished. And we will walk in more power and authority the more we view our circumstances and world through victory. Our enemy is like bread to us, so let's rise up and take back the real estate of our heart. Then we can subdue the earth and break off the curse of sin!

> *Romans 8:19-21 (TPT) "The entire universe is standing on tiptoe, yearning to see the unveiling of God's glorious sons and daughters! For against its will the universe itself has had to endure the empty futility resulting from the consequences of human sin. But now, with eager expectation, all creation longs for freedom from its slavery to decay and to experience with us the wonderful freedom coming to God's children."*

Chapter Four

OUR AUTHORITY

The amount of power and authority that God gives to us is truly incredible. To recap, we were made in God's image, fell into sin, and then were saved, healed, and restored. Part of our redemption included the gift and ability to become ONE spirit with Christ. We will never be Yahweh Himself, but we were made FROM Him. This means we have His "DNA" and are like Him. Now that we are also one with His Spirit, we can do the things that Jesus did...and greater!

> *John 14:12 (NLT) "I tell you the truth, anyone who believes in me will do the same works I have done, and even greater works, because I am going to be with the Father." [Emphasis mine]*

> *Philippians 4:13 (NLT) "For I can do everything through Christ, who gives me strength."*

We can do ANYTHING in Christ, BUT we grow into that ability. Too much power too early becomes destructive to us and to those around us. For example, let's say I had limitless power... but with an unrenewed mind. If I were to look at someone and say, *"You're crazy!"* that person would instantly be put under a spirit of crazy because I declared they were. God wields this level of power and authority, but He does not give it to us in full until we can wield it like He does. Our Father is a GOOD and WISE Father, so He set it up so that we grow our power and authority as we mature in Him.

We have a LOT of transformation to undergo before we can walk well in God's power and authority. We are born again as babies and are given power as we grow. We begin to walk in authority as we become who we are and take responsibility for our inner world. **First, we receive, then we can effectively DO.** As we learn to walk in authority in our inner world, then it will naturally translate into an outward expression.

You *can* learn to walk in a measure of authority from the outside in, but it's much slower and less effective because the power you are trying to wield is being resisted by your own soul's brokenness. Our actions do not matter as much as our soul's beliefs. It's not about what we do; it's about who we are. Man and religion are very focused on what we do, but God looks at the heart. [Matthew 23:25-28] Our actions on earth are but a vapor. What you believe and what you stand on carries more weight than your actions because the spiritual realm is the true and eternal reality we live in. This is why the spiritual realm relates to us based on what our soul BELIEVES, not by our actions or abilities. All of the spiritual realm is watching to see what we are going to believe and whose hands and feet we will manifest on the earth.

GROWING CAPACITY

I like to think of our authority in terms of capacity. All created beings have a set capacity or an amount of something they can contain. Sons of God have the capacity to walk in the power of God, but usually, the real estate (capacity) of our soul is already filled with lies and pain. Some people refer to the real estate as "thrones of the soul." Regardless of the terms we use, the reality is the same: what our soul believes matters, and it affects our capacity to walk in God's power and authority.

Matthew 6:24a (NLT) "No one can serve two masters. For you will hate one and love the other; you will be devoted to one and despise the other..."

God's truth and the lies of the enemy resist each other within our soul. They do not and cannot co-exist peacefully. Until our soul is transformed (agrees with and thinks with the mind of Christ), we will flip back and forth between a Heavenly perspective and a broken perspective. (This is why I said earlier that God's power is resisted by our soul's brokenness when we try to walk in God's power before our soul is renewed.) As we renew our minds, the real estate of our soul that once resisted God shifts into being in agreement with Him.

When I was 5, I began to be tormented by seeing demons at night. Throughout my childhood, Holy Spirit mentored me in how to have faith and taught me how to cast them out of my room. I read the Bible and learned how to "wield" the name of Jesus. After I got over the fear of seeing the demon, I would muster up the courage to face them and tell them to "leave in Jesus' name!" The demon would leave, and I would be able to sleep in peace. Without fail though, as soon as I would learn how to kick them out of my room, a bigger and more powerful demon would take its place. Each time the demons got bigger, they were scarier, and it took more courage for me to face them and kick them out.

Then one day, a demon came into my room, and I couldn't kick it out. I told it to leave in Jesus' name, and it told me that he didn't have to obey me. It sat there defiantly and confidently staring me down while I scrambled to figure out what was happening. I had always been taught that they HAVE to leave when you say "in Jesus's name." But now I had encountered a demon that told me it didn't have to leave, and I was quite shaken. It was in this season that I learned that **the spiritual realm relates to us based on our soul beliefs (capacity to carry spiritual authority), not our actions.**

This demon was more powerful than the ones I had previously encountered, and its capacity to wield spiritual power was greater than my capacity of wielding God's power. I am NOT saying that a demonic spirit is any match for Yahweh, but I was ignorant about my identity and unrenewed in my soul. My lack of faith was throttling my capacity to walk in the power and authority that I was already given.

> Mark 9:29 (ESV) "And he said to them, "This kind cannot be driven out by anything but prayer."

When the disciples couldn't kick out a demon, Jesus explained to them that this kind only comes out by prayer (and some translations include fasting). When we fast or pray, it renews our mind, which grows our capacity. I read this verse and began to fast and pray so I could kick out the demon. And sure enough, as I grew in my faith and identity and renewed my mind, I was able to kick the demon out. My capacity to wield God's power grew as I addressed unrenewed parts of my soul that were taking up voting power in my heart.

Our ability to walk in God's power again boils down to surrendering every area of our life to Yahweh. There's no way around facing our soul stuff. Our surrender and transformation are vital to our health, healing, breakthrough, maturity, and walking in authority. The dissonance in our soul fades as we align more and more with Truth. We grow our soul's capacity as we agree with and trust Yahweh more. Ultimately, we are just growing in agreement with the power of God that is already within us. As we grow and mature in the Lord, we will throttle the power of God less and less, and naturally, our lives will look more and more like Christ.

POWER COMES FROM STILLNESS

> Hebrews 3:19 (NLT) "So we see that because of their unbelief they were not able to enter his rest.

Our faith and our soul beliefs are exposed moment to moment in our circumstances. What we believe about God directly affects how we live our life. BUT... every time we lack faith in a situation, we can still renew our mind in that area of our soul and transform our life! We don't have to be stuck in the lies and dysfunction forever...we are only stuck as long as we choose to resist truth. As our faith grows, confidence in Yahweh begins to anchor our heart. The confidence/anchor we feel has many names: stillness, rest, shalom, centeredness, or peace. Stillness empowers us to be anchored in peace and make powerful choices regardless of our circumstances. Instead of being subject to circumstances or the actions and opinions of people, we can live above it all.

We are called to rule, reign, and transform the earth to look like Christ. If we live from a place of stillness, then we can make sound-minded, powerful, and Christlike choices. WE are called to define our circumstances, not to let our circumstances define our beliefs, peace, or confidence. **Power comes when our circumstances don't define our inner world.** Fear, shame, pride, or any other temptation from the enemy only have power if we agree with their lies. If we do choose the lies, then our peace is disturbed, and we are pulled out of stillness, rest, or peace.

When Jesus and the disciples were in the storm, Jesus was at rest. His confidence in Yahweh could not be shaken, even in life-threatening situations. When He and Peter needed money for taxes, again, Jesus wasn't shaken. Instead, HE defined their circumstances when He told Peter to go fishing and said a coin would be in the mouth of the fish. There is no circumstance too great, no situation too dire, that Yahweh can't fix, redeem, heal, and bring GOOD from it! Jesus was NEVER afraid. He was always at rest...confident and anchored in the goodness of God!

This is not a book (or even a chapter) on rest, so I don't want to go too deep into it. There are many things that pull us from rest, and it is vital for us to ask Jesus about them. Basically, I just want to point out some common stumbling blocks to rest. To actually get free from the blocks though, you will need to bring each block to Jesus and receive what HE says about them.

- FEAR

  o Fear pulls us from rest because we lose sight of the goodness and faithfulness of Yahweh. We then slip into striving and self-protection because we believed the lie that Yahweh didn't have us covered or provided for. Fear of pain, fear of death, fear of lack, fear of failure, and fear of rejection are the root fears that all fear stems from. [For reference, fear was talked about in-depth in Chapter 2 of Book 3 (BEcoming Whole)]

- CIRCUMSTANCES/PEOPLE

  o We give authority for people or circumstances to pull us from rest when we put our hope and expectation in them instead of Jesus. Any time we put our focus on and look to someone or something other than Yahweh, we step away from rest and step into lack. [In Chapter 2 of Book 2 (Growing in Sonship), I provided tools and teaching to empower you to be sustained IN Jesus.]

- SUFFERING

  o We will discuss this more in a few chapters, but our souls are often pulled from rest when we experience (or know of someone else experiencing) suffering. Suffering is a deeply painful and troubling reality. Most of the time, it is very hard for people to see past their emotions so that they can learn to see suffering through Jesus' eyes. More on that to come later in the book.

These stumbling blocks to rest could have been summed up to this: any agreement with a lie pulls us from rest. In reality, all of those bullet points are just different facets of our soul believing that Yahweh isn't caring for us. Any lie we believe will pull us from resting in the goodness and provision of Yahweh. The more our mind is renewed, the more at rest we will be. Stillness, or living from rest, is fundamental in sonship and is all the more important as we are trying to walk in power and authority.

While exploring rest, Jesus told me He was going to take me to "the place of His rest." When I was first taken there, I expected that "the place of His rest" was going to be a big master bedroom with an elaborate king-sized bed (because we are kings) with a pure white comforter on it (representing the Holy Spirit). I knew the Father's term "rest" does not mean "ceasing from work" or "sleeping," but that's what I expected to see when I was taken to "the place of His rest."

Instead, this room had a throne and a red robe/cape thing that was alive and represented the Holy Spirit. When I walked in, I was invited to receive the robe/cape and sit on the throne. I agreed to the invitation, and the cape immediately covered me. I then sat on the throne (which was the place of His rest). The walls turned into screens, and I could see through time and space. I saw Yahweh at work in EVERYTHING. I was in awe of the INCREDIBLE job Yahweh was doing throughout the realms. It was truly mesmerizing to see so much GOOD being woven into EVERYTHING. Once the shock of the goodness and faithfulness of God wore off a little, Holy Spirit, in the form of the robe/cape around me, then invited ME to work with Him through co-laboring and co-reigning on the earth!

I was incredibly humbled and in awe that Yahweh, God of the UNIVERSE, wanted to involve ME in the planning! My ideas were juvenile and foolish compared to His, and yet, He wove them into beautiful expressions of His goodness. He wanted this so much that He even slowed the universe down, just to include me in His process. Like a child "helping" dad on a project, I was elated to "help" bring Heaven to Earth. From the child's perspective, they don't see how much MORE time it takes to include them. But even though it was more time and work to include me, Yahweh wanted to father me in the process. *Insert crying here* I was shocked that He WANTED to include me, but once I leaned into the invitation, I had FUN working with Holy Spirit to bring Heaven to Earth. And that is when the vision ended. I had encountered "the place of His rest," and I, yet again, found God better than I had before.

The more we become convinced of the goodness of God, the more we will stay at rest in all circumstances. Trials and suffering are no match against the goodness of God. From that place of rest, we have authority over circumstances that do not sway us. The more we are anchored in Him, the less our soul will be resisting the power and authority we are wielding.

DISCERNMENT AND AUTHORITY

Recently, I found myself judging a high-profile Christian leader. Their actions were not reflecting Yahweh, and I was disgusted by how they were using their influence. I then had a come-to-Jesus moment when Yahweh said to me, "Who are you to judge a broken vessel that I chose to use?" I could have chosen to stay in judgment and be offended by what Yahweh was saying, but He has my "YES" no matter what. So, against my flesh, I chose to receive Yahweh's correction. I humbled myself and repented for judging another broken vessel because I, too, was a broken vessel and am in the beautiful process of becoming whole. In God's kindness, He gave me truth in place of my judgment. Because I chose to receive correction, my heart was springboarded into receiving revelation on the difference between discernment and judgment.

Discernment is understanding the spirit BEHIND the actions, words, or times. Discernment helps us to identify the TRUTH of information that is told to us. Whether it is someone speaking (like a sermon) or just in a conversation we are having, discernment agrees with truth and highlights/rejects things spoken out of dysfunction or pain (rooted in lies). Discernment also keeps our heart in the position of grace towards people. It separates people from their words and actions, and it helps us see people how Yahweh views them.

Judgment, however, is our ENEMY. It is a critical spirit that pulls us away from looking through the lens of grace. Without realizing it, the critical spirit pulls us into judgment over the person...because we bought the lie that "we know better than they do." It is rooted in pride and immediately stunts our growth.

Furthermore, our judgment ties the person TO their brokenness while blocking our ability to receive what God has for us. And all this happens while we think we are knowing and doing better!

While swallowing this hard pill and removing my judging lenses, I also learned that every person is dearly loved and is a unique expression of Yahweh. Regardless of their brokenness and status (*economic status and religious status*), EVERY person carries a reflection of the Father that WE can learn from. There are a few different iterations of it, but it reminds me of one of Saint Patrick's prayers:

> *Christ with me, Christ within me,*
> *Christ behind me, Christ before me,*
> *Christ beside me, Christ to win me,*
> *Christ to comfort me and restore me,*
> *Christ beneath me, Christ above me,*
> *Christ in the hearts of all that love me,*
> *Christ in the mouth of friend and stranger.*

When we are critical and judgmental towards people, we harden our heart against celebrating and receiving the image of God THEY carry because we are refusing to see them through the eyes of Love. Instead, we are invited to be humble and open so that we can see people how God sees them and discern the spirits/roots behind the scenes.

Discernment is vital in sonship. Without it, we are stunted and blinded. We also won't know when it's time to turn the other cheek or when it's time to flip some tables! Seriously though, discernment and authority go hand in hand because discernment keeps our heart softened and humbled towards the world and God. It teaches us to see the world through the eyes of Love, and then we can truly love the world as God does. Love is key to the renewal of our mind and empowers us to walk like Jesus in power on the earth.

HOW TO WALK IN AUTHORITY

Now for the nuts and bolts. In this series, we have discussed learning how to engage with Yahweh and live from Heaven to Earth. It is a process and takes time to teach our body and soul to live from the oneness that our spirit has with Jesus. In the same way, it will be a process and take time for us to learn to walk in God's authority and power. Keeping the following few things in mind is very helpful in the journey of growing in authority...

1. ENGAGE WITH YAHWEH

> *1 John 2:27 (TPT) "But the wonderful anointing you have received from God is so much greater... <u>There's no need for anyone to keep teaching you. His anointing teaches you all that you need to know</u>, for it will lead you into truth, not a counterfeit. So just as the anointing has taught you, remain in him." [Emphasis mine]*

Let us never forget: Yahweh is our eternal source and is everything we need. Engaging Yahweh seems obvious, but it's important to realize that everything flows from our connection and oneness with God. I have found it very helpful to ask Yahweh what fears or wrong mindsets are holding me back from walking in authority. I will also ask Him to show me what it looks like for me to walk in power. As I see the pictures in my mind's eye of what it looks like, then I have a blueprint for what it looks like on earth. You can ask things like:

o   What do you want to tell me about your authority and power?

o   What did it look like when Jesus walked in authority and power on earth?

o   What does it look like for me to walk in that same power and authority?

o   Are there any fears, lies, or wrong mindsets that are affecting my ability to walk in authority and power?

2. PRACTICE

It sounds funny to say "practice," but the only way to learn something new is to practice! Practice walking in authority over your body, circumstances, and nature. Speak to the weather like Jesus did. Command sickness and death to leave bodies. The only way a baby learns to walk is by trying it out. We learn by practicing. We will not walk perfectly at first. There will be lots of tripping and falling down, much like a baby does. Those moments are not failures though; they are times of learning and running to the Father for comfort.

3. LISTEN TO *(or read)* TESTIMONIES

Faith comes from hearing (Romans 10:17). Our capacity to trust Yahweh grows as we hear the testimonies of God. Since He is the same as yesterday, today, and forever, we can take confidence in the stories we hear of miracles and breakthroughs!

4. BE CHILDLIKE

Matthew 18:3-4 (TPT) "Learn this well: Unless you dramatically change your way of thinking and become teachable like a little child, you will never be able to enter in. Whoever continually humbles himself to become like this little child is the greatest one in heaven's kingdom realm."

While many of us think about spiritual things as being serious and mature subjects, Jesus made it clear that we have to be childlike to receive spiritual things. As soon as we think we know something, we stop growing! Children also have a wonderful desire to learn and explore the world around them. They are SO resilient to get up again and again after each failure. If children approached the world as adults do, they would NEVER learn to walk, talk, or mature into functioning adults. Likewise, if adults approached the world as children do, we would be quick to forgive, quick to grow, quick to try again, and quick to trust. Childlikeness is beautiful and precious, but more than that, it is vital for learning and growing in spiritual things. If being childlike wasn't important, Jesus wouldn't have mentioned it!

5. STUDY

Study what God does with His authority. Study your identity and who you are IN Christ. Study how and what other lovers of Jesus have done in the past. When we search out the scriptures, it can grow our faith as we read the testimonies of God, but also it gives us more and more of a picture of who God is and who we are.

6. STAND FIRM

I will spend an entire chapter later in this book discussing how important it is for us to stand firm. For now, just know that our choice to stand on truth in the face of adversity and trials is KEY to us seeing breakthrough and walking in authority.

All of these keys will help you in the journey of walking in authority. This journey is simple...and at the same time complicated. We can do all things in Jesus. We are one with His Spirit and will do things greater than He did. Our authority and power are being throttled by our own brokenness, but we are not stuck there. As we conquer the giants inside of us, then we can effectively conquer the giants (our enemy) in the world. (We absolutely can conquer giants in the world around us before we conquer the giants within us, but it comes at the cost of much blood, sweat, and tears because our heart is still wrestling against the truth.)

You may still be asking, "But how do I DO all the things?" That question is still rooted in doing, not in being and receiving. If power and authority are your reason for engaging with Jesus, then you have been blinded and are missing the most vital part. JESUS is our reward. And He is worth everything. The power and authority are a byproduct...not the means or cause for our intimacy with Jesus. It's not about knowledge and figuring it out. It's like a treasure hunt WITH the Father. Yahweh has concealed things FOR us to explore and discover. He does not hide things FROM us, as if He were holding back. He hides them FOR us.

> Proverbs 25:2 (BSB) "It is the glory of God to conceal a matter and the glory of kings to search it out."

> Proverbs 25:2 (TPT) "God conceals the revelation of his word in the hiding place of his glory. But the honor of kings is revealed by how they thoroughly search out the deeper meaning of all that God says."

Remember that GOD likens our relationship with Him to a marriage. The point of marriage is to live in love together happily ever after. It's not for power. It's not for figuring it out. It's not to save someone. It's not to be someone. It's not to fulfill a scroll. Marriage is for love. It's for intimacy. It's for connection. It's to be family. We were created to love and be loved. LOVE is the deepest cry of our heart. As we discover the love of God, we come alive and we can see, truly see, life as it really is. We will also walk in power and authority and mysteries beyond our wildest dreams, but they will pale in comparison to loving and being loved by Yahweh Himself.

Chapter Five

AUTHORITY AND OUR PHYSICAL BODY

As eager as we are to walk in healing and authority over our body...I can tell you right now that this isn't going where you think it is. The desire to have "authority" over our body is out of balance. I have spent over a decade trying to wrestle my body into "submission," only to have it still broken. I have fasted, blessed, rebuked, bound, released, meditated, gone to the courts, and tried natural means to heal my body...and my body STILL has issues. I did everything I knew to walk in "authority" over my body, yet it only got worse.

Until recently, I was stuck in constant frustration because I couldn't wrestle my body into "submission" and get it to reflect the healing and wholeness that Jesus paid for. There have been many layers in my transformation journey, and I am still in process! But slowly, in my soul's timing, Jesus is unraveling the mystery of my body to me. There is MUCH more to learn and grow into, but I will share with you the few things Jesus has shown me in hopes that it will bring encouragement and enlightenment to your journey with your own body. The more healing our body walks in, the easier it will be for us to do things on the earth.

Before we dive in, I want to explain that this encounter was for MY body in MY circumstance. This encounter MAY help you, but you have a different body in different circumstances. As with every element of our journey, you will need to go to Jesus about what YOUR body needs.

One day I was fasting, and I felt my body tell me that it was hungry. It's hard to explain *how* my body communicated to me... it was a voice I heard inside me, different from my soul or any other voice I have heard. (As physical as our bodies are, they are also deeply spiritual.) There was just a knowing that my physical body was talking to me. I hadn't eaten for days, and I heard my body tell me that it was hungry. My soul then responded to my body, "We are learning how to be sustained by Jesus." This was not the answer my body wanted to hear, and it quickly replied that starving it was not the way to teach it. I was both intrigued and offended, so I asked my body (with attitude), "Well then, *how* would you like to be taught?" I was not prepared for my body's reply... "Through teaching and connection!" My body then pointed out that I have been telling it for over ten years that it is healed, whole, and one with Jesus. Yet, after all this time, my body still manifests sickness, ailments, and unhealed cellular memories. My body explained that I have been harsh to it and hard on it. Even though I was making attempts to be kind to my body by giving it supplements and lots of naps, I still was very critical in my expectations and frustrations towards my body.

I knew Jesus was wanting to do something in my heart, so I took this odd conversation to Him. Fasting is good for the soul and body, so I was very confused when my body said that fasting wasn't working to "whip it into shape." Jesus then dropped the bombshell on me when He showed me a picture of my body, soul, and spirit. Without having to say a word, Jesus imparted an instant knowing (or realization) that my body, soul, and spirit were compartmentalized. So all those years while my soul was engaging with Jesus, my body was not engaging to that same level (or even at all) with Him. (My spirit is already one with Jesus and is patiently waiting for my soul and body to catch up.) Once I had the revelation of compartmentalization, I felt these blinders come off my eyes, and I could see the original intention for our bodies. I saw a beautiful oneness within our own triune being. Our body, soul, and spirit three-part being is a reflection of the three-part Godhead. Within the Godhead trinity, they are not compartmentalized or disjointed. There is perfect oneness and joy within their relationship, and that is our example!

As I simmered in this new download, I saw a vision of a martyr being tortured for Christ. To handle the pain and not deny Christ, they compartmentalized their body's pain and disconnected their soul from the body. Their soul engaged Jesus while the body underwent horrific pain. Eventually, the body gave into the agony and died. At that moment, the soul was then fully present with Jesus in the spiritual realm. There was great honor given to the martyr for their devout love and faith in Jesus. Comparatively, I then saw a picture of the Moravians. They were intimately connected with their bodies and didn't compartmentalize their body, soul, and spirit. Their bodies were joined in the bliss and oneness with Jesus like their souls were. So when people tried to kill the Moravians, they were therefore untouched and unable to be killed because their bodies were fully one with LIFE Himself.

For eternal life to transform my whole being, it was vital for me to address the compartmentalization I had done. To make it in the long run, I knew that oneness within my own three-part being was just as vital as the oneness between Jesus and my soul. Jesus then gave me four clear declarations for me to start the journey of decompartmentalizing...

1. *"I choose to forgive. From this moment forward, I choose to forget the past and the record I hold against my body."*

   - When I heard this first declaration, I felt the weight of how important it was to erase the ledger of the history and offenses I held against my body. As more history builds, more frustration and a case for accusation are built against my body. For our soul to decompartmentalize, the first step is to forgive and forget the past. This first declaration prepares the soul to be willing to receive our body instead of rejecting it in frustration.

2. *(Now talking to your body)* "*I repent for how I have treated you and for separating you from me (compartmentalizing). From here on out, things will be different. This is a U-turn in our relationship.*"

   - This declaration is now the soul addressing the body. Repent means to make a permanent change in how you think. Each time we repent, it peels one more layer off of our unrenewed mind and helps us align with the good things Jesus has for us!

3. *(Still talking to your body)* "*Body, I choose to embrace and LOVE...not just tolerate you and begrudgingly give you the basics of what you need.*"

   - This declaration realigns our soul into a healthy perspective towards our body. Self-love is a hot topic right now in Western culture...but their version of self-love is propagated by corporations trying to sell us something or by people who are grasping at straws trying to fill the missing voids in their life. Sons who love and embrace their bodies are not ONLY focused on their body's basic needs. Instead, we are on a journey of teaching our bodies how to be sustained on Heaven. Learning to love our bodies includes receiving our bodies (not rejecting them like religion taught us) and exploring how to engage Yahweh within our physical body.

4. *(Still talking to your body)* "*In place of the master-slave dynamic we had, I choose to engage you regularly and begin to develop an intimate, personal FRIENDSHIP with you.*"

   - This final declaration that Jesus gave me was something Jesus had been talking with me about for years, but it never fully clicked with my soul until this encounter. The Father, Son, and Holy Spirit have a deeply personal and blissful relationship with each other. It is a sacred and holy connection. Then God made us in their image: body, soul, and spirit. Our triune being was intended to REFLECT the Godhead's triune being, connection, and relationship.

Each part of our being is holy, sacred, and PRECIOUS to God.

(After Jesus gave me these declarations, I then made a commitment to my body that anytime I veered from this list, I would choose to return to it and renew my relationship with my body, again and again, until it reflects Jesus.)

After I had this encounter, the waves of revelation sunk deeper and deeper into my soul. Then it hit me. OF COURSE, I haven't been able to walk on water or teleport yet (something I practice/attempt regularly). How could I expect my body to do supernatural things while I was regularly rejecting it and compartmentalizing it so it wasn't encountering God? It was such a "DUH" moment that I had been totally blind to just moments before the encounter!

This chapter has probably been a lot to digest, BUT remember to digest with Jesus! Ask HIM about the encounter and what I said. Let Him sift it and reveal truth of how it applies to your soul. Decompartmentalizing and teaching our body to live from Heaven will take time, but it is a beautiful part of our journey! There are many lies to be revealed and many adjustments for our soul to make in order for us to have a deep and personal friendship within our own three-part being.

THE LIES

In this journey of embracing our bodies, I want to address how much religion has perverted the way we view our physical bodies. They are made in the image of Yahweh Himself, and they are incredible! Our bodies are the highest technology created in this dimension on earth. Unfortunately, religion teaches that the body is a ragged tent that we will be free from one day. It tells us that we are just biding our time on earth till we can escape to Heaven and that the shell of our body is just the vehicle we drive until we die. Religion claims that it doesn't matter and isn't eternal. It spiritualizes and glorifies the running of our bodies into the ground to fulfill our religious duties while on earth. How sad and how blind we have been!

The gospel is not about escaping the earth; it is about TRANSFORMING the earth to look like Heaven! Furthermore, Jesus came to redeem and heal the BODY! Then He took His BODY with Him when He ascended! (Enoch and Elijah also took their bodies when they skipped death and ascended into Heaven!) Our bodies are a sign and a wonder. They have multi-dimensional capabilities and can break the rules of the physical dimension that they were formed in!!! Truly unique to all of creation, our body is a temple capable of holding the Spirit of Yahweh. The rest of creation can have the Spirit of God rest ON them, but we get to have the Spirit of God IN us, ONE with us.

To address the lies and wrong perspectives we have, we of course ask Jesus about it! You can ask things like:

- That was a strange encounter Jessica just shared...what do you say about it?

- What do YOU think about my body?

- What does a healthy relationship within my body, soul, and spirit look like?

- How do I start the journey of having a personal relationship with my body?

- And how do I talk with my body?

- How do I decompartmentalize my body, soul, and spirit?

Important note: it's not about just hearing the answers from Jesus. Hearing does nothing unless we act on it (James 1:22). Once Jesus reveals any lies or wrong beliefs, then break agreement with them, and make a conscious choice to receive what Jesus says in their place. As with other areas of renewing the mind (talked about in-depth in Becoming Whole [Book 3]): identify, break agreement, and receive!

Transforming the perception we have of our body takes time... beautiful time that we get to spend growing our trust and friendship with Jesus, and beautiful time that we get to spend repairing the relationship we have with our own body. The questions listed above are intended to be done over time, not all at once.

HEALING CELLULAR MEMORY

As physical as our bodies are, they are also spiritual and emotional. While on this journey of oneness, I want to add one more piece: understanding cellular memory. A body has (on average) around 37 TRILLION cells. More impressive is that our cells have the ability to remember things and store data; this is known as cellular memory.

There have been MANY cases when organ transplant recipients have personality changes, memories, or reoccurring dreams after receiving an organ. From what scientists have been able to tell, the cellular memory in the donated organ was able to transfer stored data to the recipient's body! It has been reported that after the surgery, some recipients have experienced changes in mood, behaviors, food preferences, cravings, music, art, and recreational or career preferences. Some of the most bizarre occurrences have been recipients that suddenly wake up with the ability to play an instrument, speak a new language, or even have their blood type change!

Even more impressive was the lab rat study done on cellular memory. To study the effects of cellular memory, scientists took a lab rat and would introduce a specific smell to it while at the same time shocking its feet. They did this repeatedly to the rat so that the smell was always correlated with the pain of the shock. Then the scientists began to just introduce the smell to the rat without giving the shock, and the rat's body would have the same neurological response as if it were shocked! To take the study one step further, they took the seed of the rat and impregnated a rat at a different facility with it. There was no interaction between the father and offspring because they were at different labs. They then introduced the offspring to the same smell but with NO shock. To their surprise, the offspring had a fearful, neurological response to the smell even though the offspring had never been shocked before! The response was not as intense as it was for the father rat, but the experiment proved that cellular memory can be passed on! The experiment then continued on for one more generation. Incredibly, the second generation of rats also had a fear response even though they never had been shocked!

Studying cellular memory is a bizarre but impressive ride. I brought up cellular memory because it validates the necessity to take your body on encounters with Jesus. Our bodies keep score and remember more than we imagine!

Furthermore, Dr. Caroline Leaf has been able to scientifically prove that our bodies manifest or reflect the soul's beliefs and health. 6 times a minute (every 10 seconds) our physical brain syncs up with our soul and manifests the soul's beliefs. This means that as our soul heals, our body can heal! While this is true, I have found that there were times when my body still needed healing, even after my soul healed. In those circumstances, my body chose to hold on to the trauma and its effects even though my soul chose to heal. For example, after spending years going on inner healing encounters with Jesus, I was free from all of the sexual abuse ripples in my life...or so I thought. The night terrors, insecurities, and extreme fears were gone! I was free! Until I started dating my husband...then when he would innocently reach for me or touch my wrist, it would shut my body down and send me immediately into a traumatic memory. It was during this season of my life that I first learned about cellular memory. My soul was showing no more signs of trauma and wounds, but my body was still carrying the memories of my past.

Each time I was triggered and sent back into a memory, I took time to talk to my body and bring the memory to Jesus. I would say something like:

1. Body, I call you to attention, and I bless you to hear and receive truth right now.

2. I bless my cells to open up and release every toxin, negative memory, and evil thing. You don't have to carry them anymore, and in their place, I bless you to receive the healing and truth of Jesus.

3. Body, I bless you to know that you are safe. You are loved, and you are appreciated. (You can begin to talk with your body about an event that it is feeling traumatized about. Tell your body out loud, that it was never God's plan for it to endure "XYZ" [the trauma or pain it went through].)

4. Jesus, I ask that you heal every trauma and negative memory in my cells. Please restore my cells to the original design You had planned for them.

5. Thank You Jesus for healing my body and thank you body for opening up and receiving this encounter.

I mentioned at the beginning of the chapter that my body, soul, and spirit were compartmentalized, so you may be wondering how that happened if I was taking my body on encounters with Jesus. I took my body on encounters YEARS ago. After the cellular memories from the abuse were gone, I went back to normal living. I still compartmentalized and was still trying to muscle my body into being healed and whole. It wasn't until recently that I understood the oneness available to us within our own three-part being, and I definitely didn't realize that I was leaving my body out of the encounters and journey I was on with Jesus. But that's just it, it's part of the love dance. We are in a beautiful process with Jesus. Remember that it is not about figuring it out. We aren't trying to arrive at some spiritual destination. We have joined in the love dance and relationship with the Trinity. Learning how to decompartmentalize our triune being and learning how to enable our body to engage Jesus is just part of our process! So ask Jesus questions, explore, and be patient!

Chapter Six

STANDING FIRM

In this wild journey of sonship, I have seen tsunamis and tornados miraculously be dissolved. I have stopped miscarriages, seen healings, cast out demons, shifted atmospheres, changed the past and the future, and many other odd things. Simultaneously... I have prayed for many healings and miracles and they did NOT come to pass. I also have prayed for the resurrection of many dead friends and family members, and none of them have come back to life. I wasn't able to stop my own miscarriage, and I have seen lots and lots of times when "it didn't work."

> Psalm 27:13 (AMP) "I would have despaired had I not believed that I would see the goodness of the LORD In the land of the living."

Standing firm. Having grit. Getting back up after being kicked down. Deciding who you are in the darkest moments. THOSE are the moments that reveal who we are at our core and what we will stand for. When my baby died, when my friends and relatives got sick and died, when my bills went unpaid, when I had a complete psychological breakdown and couldn't function at all, when all hope was lost, when there was no light at the end of the tunnel, and when the only thing I could hear were the voices of my accusers...I had a decision to make. Would I buckle under the pressure? Would I harden my heart against God? Would I give up on my faith altogether? THIS is the elephant in the room that I want to address in this chapter. What about the times we don't see the breakthrough or healing? What about the prophecies that don't come true? What gives? How do we move on from the pain and disappointment? When do we "take a loss," and when do we keep standing? These are all very big and painful questions that pretty much everyone asks.

It is at these moments that many believers give up. They quit pressing in, and they settle for a simple Christian life...or they lose their faith altogether. Lots of people give up when they face hardship. Since there is no shame or condemnation for those in Christ, it actually is "legal" for someone to quit pressing in and settle. BUT when we choose that, we stunt our growth. Because of Jesus, we can choose to push past our offense and not get stuck. And if we do, we will find breakthrough and healing on the other side of our offense.

Pastors and speakers love to talk about miracles and breakthroughs, but rarely do they share about the losses, unfulfilled dreams, and prayers that felt unanswered. If we don't talk about the hard times, people can easily become dismayed, confused, and troubled when they face their own unfulfilled dreams and hardships. While we want to help prepare the believers for hard times, there are no "easy" answers to "Why didn't it work?" and for the loss we feel. Life on earth is hard. It would be nice if there were quick answers, fixes, or formulas that we could apply to "figure out" how to walk the walk. But that is not how it works. There are many factors that affect our life on earth, and most of those factors can't be manipulated into a desired outcome.

This is my process when I am trying to sort out times when "It didn't work"

1. The first place to start, as always, is by bringing the frustration, pain, and disappointment to Jesus.

   • Surrender is always key. In our pain, it is easy to spin out in offense and confusion. When our loved ones die, when hopes are lost, or when we feel abandoned by God, those are the times that many people break and stop standing firm. Staying close to Jesus is vital for life, but it is especially vital during hard times.

2. After the surrender (and coming to terms with whatever I am facing), I give my heart time to grieve.

- In Chapter 6 of Book 3 (BEcoming Whole), I explained how grieving is a gift from Jesus. Grieving is the way our heart heals from pain, and it keeps us from being crushed by the weight of life's many tragedies. When we don't grieve, our soul becomes stuck in pain, frustration, and confusion. If we are not intentional to receive Jesus' healing in the painful areas of our hearts, then we will live our lives in continual reaction to those past wounds.

3. Once my heart is no longer crushed from the pain, I ask Jesus for HIS perspective. *(You don't have to wait for all of the pain to be healed. I give my heart time to grieve so that I am no longer drowning in it. When I can think of something other than the pain, then my heart is in a better place to hear from Jesus about what He thinks and see His perspective)*

- Seeing things from Heaven's perspective brings comfort to our hurting soul. Heaven's perspective IS the true reality, and we have the ability to live from Heaven to Earth in all we do. Truth is truth beyond physical facts and time. Seeing our painful events through Jesus' perspective brings healing. (More on seeing things from Heaven's perspective will be discussed later in this book)

The quote that comes to mind is, "Where else can we go? Only You have the words of life." The disciples said this right after Jesus told the crowd to eat His flesh and drink His blood. Everyone left except them. They just stood there...bewildered by the blasphemous and horrendous *sounding* things they just heard JESUS Himself say. They couldn't make sense of what He said, BUT they knew that Jesus was the way, the truth, and life. Even when He offended them and was WAY outside their box, they chose to cling to Him in the midst of the unknown.

The same choice is before us. We can be offended that God didn't do or say what we wanted Him to, or we can choose Him in the midst of the confusion and pain. When facing the pain and confusion of "it's not working," what our heart needs more than anything is to be close to Jesus. As much as we may feel desperate to have answers...answers cannot heal our hearts. *"Where else can we go?"* is still true for us today. Clinging to and choosing Jesus is the only way, the only truth, and the only life.

THE TENSION OF STANDING FIRM

Let's talk about dead raising. There are testimonies of people who were dead for YEARS, decades even, that came back to life when someone prayed over them. So when praying to raise the dead, how long "should" you pray? How long do you keep standing in faith, and when do you decide to stop praying and bury the body? There is no cookie-cutter answer for questions like these. This is why learning how to stand firm is so complicated. On one hand, our hope and trust are in Jesus BEYOND our circumstances and desires. On the other hand, we are called to transform the whole earth, rule, and reign....which includes dreams and desiring things on the earth. So how do we dream while keeping our hope in Jesus? Dreaming and standing firm *seem* to be contradicting concepts. This is the *tension* of standing firm.

I would love to provide steps and formulas to walking in sonship and authority, but there is just no such thing. There isn't an exact number of hours that you must pray to bring someone back from the dead...or an exact formula for performing any miracle. There are many, many mighty men and women of God who move strongly in healing, and in spite of all their "successes," they still don't see every person healed...or sometimes they themselves are sick. I wholeheartedly believe that we all can grow to be as capable in healing as Jesus was. (*Remember that Jesus Himself said, "Greater things you shall do!"*) At the same time, I recognize we are in the process of becoming as proficient in miracles as Jesus was.

The best way I can describe the answer to the tension is to walk in surrender and stand firm simultaneously. It's wholeheartedly believing for something...while at the same time leaving it in the hands of Jesus. My hope and faith continually remain in Jesus while I practice taking responsibility and attempting to bring Heaven to Earth. I think of it as staying firmly grounded IN Christ while we are learning how to "ride the bike" of sonship. Each attempt to walk in power and authority is simply an attempt to "ride the bike." We are NOT the savior, nor will we ever be. We are not Jesus. We are CHILDREN of Yahweh who are learning how to grow up into mature sonship. And until we are glowing like a lightbulb (*AKA transfigured...totally renewed in our mind*), we are still just KIDS in the process of learning the family business.

The ONLY answer to this tension is to talk to Jesus. I hope by now you have recognized the pattern in this series. Go. To. Jesus. HE has all the answers and can answer these deep, painful questions in ways that words on a page never can. He will tell you when it is time to keep praying and when it is time to bury the body.

After your heart has surrendered and grieved, your heart is in a better place to receive from Jesus. It is important not to make an idol out of "needing" answers from Jesus. As long as the questions are not an idol, Jesus can use the answers to launch us into more freedom and wholeness. Here are some examples of great questions to ask:

- What do you want to tell me about_____? (Sometimes indirect questions help the soul stay in a heart posture that is easier to receive)

- How do I know when to keep believing for something or when it is time to surrender_____ back to you?

- How do YOU see this situation?

The more flustered our soul is, the more difficult it is to hear an answer from Jesus in the midst of the whirling emotions. It may take a while for our soul to heal and recover enough for us to hear an answer from Jesus. When pressing in for a miracle, it may feel like you don't have time to wait to hear an answer. "*I need an answer NOW. I'm facing a crisis!*" Those are the times when trust can be the hardest. Even though we may be in crisis, Jesus is not in crisis, and HE gets the final say. He promises to bring GOOD in ALL things. In the midst of the chaos and emotion, Jesus continually invites us to enter into His rest. I will go more in-depth later in this book, but I will share a few truths that I use to anchor myself in crisis:

o   When all we see is our pain, we lose sight of Jesus.

o   Remember that Jesus is ONE with you.

o   He IS speaking and has not abandoned you in your pain.

o   As we grieve and allow the pain to heal, our soul will become more and more able to receive what Jesus is already saying.

o   Jesus is big enough to bring good from EVERY thing we face.

When facing a crisis, it can be very hard to discern when to stop believing for a miracle and when to keep standing in faith. We don't ever want to give up. Giving up is when we quit because we have lost hope. What I am talking about is powerfully choosing to stop contending for a miracle so that we stay in rest and don't slip into striving. Often what we are contending for becomes an idol to us. When our hearts are still, we can more effectively hear when to keep contending and when to surrender it to Jesus. Basically, cling to Jesus in all things and at all times, and as your soul grows capacity, you will be able to hear what Jesus is already speaking to you. He is our anchor in the tension of contending or surrendering.

GROWING IN GRIT

As you probably have experienced, walking this life out is very different than how we imagined it would be. Interestingly, the hard times reveal what our soul truly believes and the depth of our grit. (Grit means courage, resolve, or the strength of character.) For example, Peter was adamant that he would never deny Jesus...but just shortly after saying that, Peter caved to fear. He didn't have the grit to follow through. We can hope that we will stand firm, but there's no way to know what we are actually going to do...until we face hard times. Thanks to Yahweh's moment-to-moment redemption, if we do respond soulishly to something, we can course correct at any time! We are presently and continually deciding what type of person we will be. We may not have had courage or grit in the past, but in an instant, we can course correct and choose Jesus over fear.

The cool thing is that even having grit (standing firm) is designed to be done WITH Jesus. We can't strive enough in our own strength to produce the fruit we want to see in our life. To see good fruit, we simply abide in (live from) the Tree of Life! (Remember, Jesus is the vine, and we are the branches!) We can't be strong enough on our own. Even standing firm in our own strength brings death. JESUS empowers us with strength and courage ALL the time (which includes hard times). It is HIS strength we are relying on, not ours. Again, it comes down to OUR choice to choose Him and rely on His strength in the hard times. The more we choose Jesus over fear, the more we will walk in HIS strength and grit.

Many people quit and give up when faced with this tension. They think "it didn't work" and then build a theology around the experience. This happens when we harden our heart in the face of crisis. It is a natural response to let our pain define us and/ or what we believe. BUT we can have a supernatural response and allow what Jesus says to define our pain. THAT is when everything changes. As painful as the crisis is, it will always be less painful the closer we walk with Jesus. It takes grit to cling to Jesus in the midst of the pain, but it is ALWAYS worth the cost. And you CAN cling to Him if you rely on His strength.

BECOMING UNSHAKABLE

Jesus was unshakable in every circumstance He faced. He ALWAYS chose to live from Heaven's reality. And since truth SUPERECEDES facts, Jesus was never shaken by the circumstances He faced. His peace, joy, and confidence in

Yahweh were unshakeable. This means that it is possible for us to grow into becoming unshakable and be able to stand firm no matter the circumstance. He didn't react to the enemy and pain. Instead, Jesus only did what He saw the Father doing. As long as we live in reaction to pain, then we will be hindered in authority and power over the circumstance. Our ability to stand firm comes down to our ability to live from Heaven (relying on Jesus' strength). "Come up here" is the invitation of the gospel. As we live FROM Heaven, everything becomes clear. Our burden is light. We have infinite strength and grit IN Jesus. We are fully convinced of the goodness of God, and we...fear...nothing... EVER!

No one can escape suffering and pain because we all live in this broken world. Creation is waiting for the sons of God to transform and redeem the earth. That is the plan that we are waking up to and walking towards, but our current reality still has suffering and pain. Later in the book, we will explore how fearing pain blocks our ability to see pain through Heaven's eyes. In this section, I am wanting to empower you to start learning how to live unshakeable in the midst of the brokenness in this world. As long as WE are dismayed by, dismissing of, or fixated on the brokenness in this world, WE will be subject to pain and stunted from walking in authority. Sons of God are able to walk in believing for creation's transformation while at the same time being at rest with its broken state. We can have confidence that God is working in the midst of the suffering. The more we see Heaven's perspective, the more our heart will be unshakeable instead of dismayed and shaken by the pain we encounter.

Being at peace with the status of the world does NOT mean we (or God) are ok with the status of the world. We are not "accepting" pain and suffering to just "go along and get along." It is NOT a form of powerlessness and giving up...instead, we are freeing ourselves from negative emotions (that aren't in Heaven!) and are aligning ourselves with God's perspective. It is THE most powerful place for our soul to be.

When I am not under the influence of something (like not

living in reaction to pain for example), then my soul is able to have authority over that very thing. If it doesn't rule over my emotions, then I can rule over it. Likewise, I can't have authority over anything my soul is <u>reactionary</u> about. Jesus did not react to pain, instead, He lived in response to the Father. Being at rest with the status of the world comes from JESUS carrying my burdens, from seeing things through Heaven's eyes, and through, of course, intimacy with Jesus.

As we become unshakable, we are able to stand firm in ALL things (because we are living from Heaven towards Earth). Furthermore...we become an unstoppable force, just like Jesus, because we are walking in the empowerment and authority of Yahweh. Until then, cling to Jesus in all things and in all circumstances. Every trigger is an invitation to breakthrough! If we don't harden our heart in the pain, we will find healing and growth in Jesus. And that healing and growth will produce a beautiful maturity as we become more like Jesus.

> *James 1:2-4 (TPT) "My fellow believers, when it seems as though you are facing nothing but difficulties, see it as an invaluable opportunity to experience the greatest joy that you can! For you know that when your faith is tested it stirs up in you the power of endurance. And then as your endurance grows even stronger, it will release perfection into every part of your being until there is nothing missing and nothing lacking."*

Chapter Seven

MONEY, MONEY, MONEY

Even though money isn't directly correlated to authority, money is considered "power," so I wanted to address money in this book. It is a painful and frustrating subject for most people as they navigate life. So much emotion is spent worrying about money and trying to figure out how to make it or grow it. Money is an idol for most people, believers included. *I define an idol as a person or thing that has a lot of emotion (good or bad) invested into it.* Idols are interesting because we blindly enslave ourselves to what we are idolizing and fight to protect the very thing we are bound to. In regards to money, it is an idol to most people because we are constantly weighing, measuring, and concerned about it. Below are some questions you could ask yourself to see if money has a hold on your heart...

- Do you worry about whether there will be enough money?

- Do you wish you could win the lottery because it would *"make life easier"*?

- Do you think that if you had enough money, you would be happy or at peace?

- Do you strive to be a good *"steward"* of your finances out of fear?

- Do you see your abundance or lack of money as a reflection of your faith or what God thinks of you?

Everyone is affected by money. This worldly system is run by various forms of money or resources. To live in this world is to be subject to that money system...until we transfigure out of it! (*We will talk about that in a bit!*) Because money is the currency of this realm, it is a source of torment for most people. They are trapped in that system and look to money as their SOURCE. From a natural perspective, money is the source of provision, source of identity, source of success, source of comfort, and source of value. Most "spiritual" people and religions have gotten caught up in the world's perspective of money. Even in Christianity, there are many opposing thoughts/beliefs about money and what believers "should" think about it.

RELIGION AND MONEY

In regards to money, there are two common camps/variations taught in religion:

- Some sects of religion teach that God doesn't want you to have money. "*It's the root of all evil. Live a bare minimum life and give everything that you don't need to the poor. You're just a wretch anyways. To be a good Christian, you must live humbly, and your humility is reflected not just in your actions but also in your belongings. Poverty is a form of spirituality. Grovel, serve, repeat!*"

- Other sects of religion teach that "*God wants to bless you beyond your wildest dreams! Be sure to tithe, be a good Christian, and God WILL richly bless you. The more blessings you have reflects your faith, how good of a Christian you are, and how pleased God is with you. You are kings and queens! Remember that the wealth of the wicked is stored up for YOU! Wealth is a form of spirituality. Tithe, receive His grace, and reap!*"

You have probably heard of these two camps or something along the same lines. So much judgment, fear, and condemnation have been wrapped up in this topic of money. Notice that BOTH camps have *some* truth wiggled in. Jesus *did* ask one man to sell all his belongings. We *are* kings and queens. So where is the balance?

Is money evil, or is money a blessing? I want to propose to you that money is...neither! It is a NEUTRAL resource on the earth that can bring good or devastation. Every resource on this earth is but dust...the gold, land, and money (paper or digital). All of it is all able to be taken away in an instant. All earthly wealth is temporary and fleeting. It IS all for nothing...like the paper money in the Monopoly game.

The question for us is...HOW can we live from Heaven (be a multidimensional being) while existing in a world run by money? As sons, our SOURCE is Yahweh, and our home and identity come from Heaven. Heaven supersedes the physical realm, BUT we still are plugged into this dirt world. From Heaven's perspective, what we know as "reality" in this physical realm is just a vapor made of sound waves. [*See Chapter 7 of Book 2 (Growing in Sonship) for sound wave reference.*] During this short time on earth, having "Monopoly" money *is* nice. It is *nice* to be able to buy and do whatever we want. In the big picture though...how much money we have or don't have doesn't matter in Heaven. It's all just sound waves. The "Monopoly" money of this world does not convert into a spiritual reality when we die. So does money matter at all? No...and yes. Let's dive in deeper...

WHAT DOES GOD THINK?

We know that God (Father, Son, and Holy Spirit) are all intimately entangled within the fabric of our physical dimension, BUT there is nothing God needs from it. He does not need our money, our time, or any other resource. HE is the source for all of creation. That being said, our money doesn't affect God at all...in one way or another. Why then did Jesus talk about money one-third of the time in His parables? Because money greatly affects OUR hearts...

> *Luke 12:15 (TPT) "Speaking to the people, Jesus continued, "Be alert and guard your heart from greed and from always wishing for what you don't have. For your life can never be measured by the amount of things you possess."*

Growing up in religion, I was told that God cared about money. Since I never questioned it and asked Jesus Himself about it, I spent years striving and stressing over money and wanting to please God. Before we discuss authority over money, I would like to dismantle a few of the lies that religion propagates.

RELIGION'S MONEY PROPAGANDA #1

"God doesn't want you to have money because the love of money is the root of all evil."

> Jesus did tell the rich young ruler to sell all he owned. Jesus knew the bondage of the young man who asked to follow Him, and He was inviting him to be FREE of his bondage. The love of money destroys us, and Jesus was giving him a choice...the choice between money and LIFE. If God truly didn't want us to have money, then He would not have made King Solomon the wealthiest man on the planet. Money doesn't matter, it's just another resource. So having money, or not having it, doesn't matter...what DOES matter is if money has our heart.

RELIGION'S MONEY PROPAGANDA #2

"God wants to bless you beyond your wildest dreams! Be sure to tithe, be a good Christian, and God WILL richly bless you. The more blessings you have reflects your faith, how good of a Christian you are, and how pleased God is with you."

> God DOES love His kids, and He is a GOOD Father. Every parent loves to bless their children, but monetary things are not the ultimate blessing...they can even be a curse at times. Remember that God has already blessed us with EVERY spiritual blessing (Eph 1:3). To focus on monetary blessing is a trap for our soul and shifts our gaze from Jesus onto shallow and temporary physical things.

RELIGION'S MONEY PROPAGANDA #3

"God wants to bless us financially, but He won't give it to us until we can steward it well. It is His kindness to not give us abundant finances prematurely because we would squander it with our brokenness."

I do agree that God doesn't give us things prematurely. For example, a car would be an instrument of death if given to a child. So, in that aspect, that part is true. It IS His kindness to not give us things that we are not ready for. That being said...the idea that "God is holding out on giving you financial abundance until you are mature enough to steward it" is an ambiguous place to put ourselves in. Each person's definition of "abundant finances" will be different from their neighbor's. Self-created definitions are a COMMON delusion our souls live in. The abundant life we live in is not weighed and measured in monetary value. We may have money, or money may be lacking; either way, our Heavenly identity, place, and value are unchanging. Earthly abundance is money. Heavenly abundance is Jesus.

If maturity equaled abundant finances...we would expect Jesus to have been bursting at the seams with money, especially during the peak of His ministry. Jesus *may* have been rich, but scripture is unclear. Religious scholars are divided about Jesus' economic status. Regardless, we do see many times in scripture that "abundant finances" were not present. Jesus turned water into wine, multiplied food, and created money out of thin air with the money fish. Again and again, Jesus did miracles to provide for needs because, from what we can tell, there weren't "abundant finances" present. We see the same thing in the lives of the generals of faith throughout history. There rarely was what our soul would define as "abundant finances" present in their lives and ministries. If the generals of the faith and Jesus Himself didn't have unlimited money VISIBLE to them...then abundant life and provision are not measured in monetary presence, AND monetary presence is not an indication of spiritual maturity.

Philippians 4:11-14 (BSB) "I am not saying this out of need, for I have learned to be content regardless of my circumstances. I know how to live humbly, and I know how to abound. I am accustomed to any and every situation — to being filled and being hungry, to having plenty and having need. I can do all things through Christ who gives me strength."

RELIGION'S MONEY PROPAGANDA #4

"You MUST tithe to be a good Christian."

If your hair wasn't raised yet, they probably are now! Tithing IS an Old Testament law...and I want to submit to you that it is part of the law that Jesus fulfilled. We don't live under the OLD covenant anymore. We got a better deal, at a higher cost. We DIED and were given the Kingdom. You may think, "Yay! I don't have to tithe anymore." Not quite...now EVERYTHING you are and have belongs to Jesus. Before, we owed God 10%, but now you are ONE spirit with Him. Tithing is not a New Testament command because we are living sacrifices. We are Christ in the flesh on the earth. It's His money. It's no longer about weighing and measuring 10% to fulfill the law. It's about being made one in a marriage, and 100% of what is yours is now Christ's...and vice versa.

RELIGION'S MONEY PROPAGANDA #5

"Debt is bad, so you shouldn't go into debt. God wants us to be good stewards of our money, and debt is irresponsible."

There is a lot of religious pressure to be a "good steward." Religion says that we must always be working and striving to be "good enough" according to whatever religious standard we are a part of. This striving to be "good enough" and a "good steward" is rooted in weighing and measuring our life according to our *knowledge* of good and evil. But we didn't get saved INTO religion or the Tree of Knowledge! Our gospel is not about us striving to measure up! Jesus did what we could not and now all we have to do is RECEIVE what HE did! Our gospel is about doing things WITH the Father. SONship is about relationship! HE will teach us how to mature and be like Him (which includes stewardship but there is SO much more for us to grow in). **We are missing the point of the gospel anytime we are striving to do things in our own strength (including being a "good steward").** In fact, there is DEATH in our striving to be good enough because we are doing things from our knowledge of good and evil!

Now regarding debt, the Old Testament DOES speak a lot about debt, and in Romans, Paul encourages us to not let our debt go outstanding. What the Bible says IS true. Period. The problem is that most believers have become very legalistic in their views toward what the Bible says, and in this context, their views on debt. It's important to remember that we are not under the law anymore (legalism included). We are sons that live under a new covenant, and our new covenant focuses on the HEART.

A debt MINDSET is destructive and not a Kingdom mindset. EQUALLY true, a legalistic mindset is ALSO destructive and not a kingdom mindset. In reality, the amount of debt or wealth of "Monopoly" money we have does not matter in Heaven. This is all a vapor and the things of this life are but dust. What matters is the heart. God does not care how much "dust" we have or how much "dust" we owe...and that is all it truly is.

Furthermore, in our new covenant, "*everything is now permissible, but not everything is beneficial*" (1 Cor 10:23). This is a VERY uncomfortable concept the first several times hearing it. We are CONSTANTLY (subconsciously) measuring "right and wrong" from the Tree of Knowledge. In the next chapter, we will dive into this whole topic, so hold tight for more explanation on this. For now, I am making the point that debt itself is inconsequential from

Heaven's perspective, what matters is the HEART behind and towards debt.

ALL of this propaganda we just discussed had *partial* truths woven into it. Those partial truths were then further filtered through our soul wounds and lies. They then became death and bondage to us because we didn't stop to ask Jesus what He thought. Any time we do things on our own, we make a mess and miss the point. I encourage you to take every religious concept of money to Jesus. Ask Jesus what HE thinks, and you will find yourself just as surprised as I was!

In the big picture, money is nothing more than a tool for us to use during the vapor we are here. The amount of "Monopoly" money we have is not a reflection of Yahweh and His goodness. He is good regardless of how this vapor turns out. Likewise, the amount of money we have or don't have is not a direct reflection of our faith, favor, or success. Our soul beliefs absolutely affect our finances, but our debt or abundance is not "proof" of our spiritual capacity.

I believe that Yahweh is not <u>concerned</u> about our debt, nor is He <u>proud</u> of our monetary success. If He were proud of monetary success or concerned about debt, that would train us to care about temporary resources during this vapor. I am not saying that Yahweh doesn't care about our physical well-being, but rather that Yahweh is constantly inviting us to live from a higher reality above the dust.

AUTHORITY OVER MONEY

As multi-dimensional beings, the presence or lack of money does affect our natural lives and how we live. But remember that our natural lives are a vapor. The amount of Monopoly money you have while playing the game does affect the game, but it is not lasting. In the big picture, it doesn't matter. All of "your" money can vanish in an instant. You have no control over it. Natural disasters can destroy your possessions. Governments can steal your land. Everything you have worked hard for can disappear. It is all but dust, none of it translating over through the veil.

What matters is the heart. THAT is what God cares about because it is eternal. God "cares" about money only because of the way it affects our soul! Our response to money shows if we are living from Heaven toward Earth or if we have succumbed to the world's ideology.

Quick note...giving credit to Yahweh for the provision of your finances does NOT prevent your heart from looking at money as an idol. If I am excited about or disgusted by money, it reveals a hold on me. As long as money affects our emotions, IT has authority over us. To walk in authority OVER money, our soul must be free from fear and love of money. Once we are indifferent to it, like we would be in a Monopoly game, then we are truly free.

If we don't learn to be content IN Jesus, then the enemy will make sure that there will NEVER be enough. When our peace, joy, and contentment are in any way attached to money, we open the door to being continually tormented by the enemy. Please remember that we NEVER benefit from partnering with lies from the enemy...all we get in return is death disguised as a pseudo-benefit.

> Philippians 4:11b (BSB) "I have learned to be content regardless of my circumstances."

Money can either be a tool that we use, OR it can be something we are enslaved to and live under. It becomes an idol anytime we look at money as anything more than a tool. It does not and cannot bring contentment, peace, or joy. Yahweh is our source for all life, peace, joy, contentment, AND provision. We do NOT need money. We can do great things and be about kingdom work without a single penny. God is not limited or throttled by money...and neither are we! But we *can* become throttled by money...when we forget our identity and fall into the Monopoly game ideology.

We don't have authority over things that rule over our heart. To have authority over money, we can't be affected by money! So how do we get free? Jesus is the quick and easy answer of course, but it might not be quick and easy to change the way our soul views money. We have been SO indoctrinated with how to view and relate to money. Regardless of what our beliefs are, money is deeply woven into our concepts of identity, provision, comfort, etc. Usually, it will take time for our soul to be willing to receive what Jesus says about the "Monopoly" money. Below are some great questions you can ask Him to jumpstart the journey...

- What do YOU say about all this madness Jessica just spewed?

- What lies am I believing about money?

- What is the currency of Heaven?

- How do I live from Heaven to Earth while still living on Earth?

In this chapter, I intentionally didn't cover every verse and every concept regarding money. You probably have lots of questions, which is great! Go talk to Jesus about them. He is our source and can show you the truth in ways I never can.

Chapter Eight

LIVING FROM THE TREE OF LIFE

Everything Yahweh does revolves around RELATIONSHIP. In order to give us true freedom, God gave us the ability to reject Him, which includes rejecting LIFE. In the garden, Yahweh created two trees that stood apart from the rest: the Tree of Life, (which was a tangible manifestation of God's abundant life) and the Tree of Knowledge of good and evil (which was the tangible manifestation of our ability to reject God). In the garden, there was no law. There was only abundant life and the command to not eat of the Tree of Knowledge which represented our choice to do things without God, in our own strength. For the majority of this series, I have used the term "choose Jesus," but really, it's the same thing as choosing the Tree of Life.

Adam and Eve had a clear and tangible choice presented to them in the garden. Adam and Eve were not convinced of the goodness of God. So when they were tempted to be like God, they rejected God's abundant life and tried to accomplish for themselves...what they already had. They were duped, but they were duped because they didn't ask Yahweh about it. They didn't invite Him into the conversation. Instead, they tried to do it in their own strength, and in doing so, they rejected and disobeyed God.

The Tree of Life (choose Jesus/do things with Him) and the Tree of Knowledge (don't choose Jesus/do things in your own strength) are the same choices we have today. For us, the trees are no longer tangible. Nevertheless, from moment to moment, we choose which tree our heart will operate from. Because they are no longer tangible choices, the hard part for us is RECOGNIZING their reality. All we have ever known was how to subconsciously think and live from the Tree of Knowledge. The moment we chose Jesus, we became one SPIRIT with Him, but our SOUL remains unrenewed. Our soul is the house of our free will, so that is why we are responsible for the renewal of our minds. This means that, even as believers, we remain deeply entrenched in the Tree of Knowledge until we break agreement with the old mindsets and choose Jesus in EVERY area of our lives.

As sons of God, we aren't TRYING to reject God. We love God and want to eat from the Tree of Life...but our understanding of how to live "right" comes from our knowledge of good and evil. We are constantly weighing, measuring, and judging what is "good" and "evil." The problem is that we are striving to do life in OUR strength and understanding. The moment we do anything separate from Yahweh (eat of the Tree of Knowledge) is the moment we start to wither...like a vine cut off the branch.

Adam and Eve (obviously) believed in God, BUT that belief wasn't enough for them to choose to obey God in all things. Similarly, we believe in God, but we are not convinced of His goodness. This leads to us using our twisted "understanding" of "good" and "evil" to navigate life, even after being saved. Instead of striving and trying to figure it out, **the Tree of Life is all about ONENESS.** Restoring oneness is a core concept of the gospel. We are invited to live from the Tree of Life, which simply looks like holding our loving Father's hand while we learn how to walk WITH Him. He is the Father, which means HE guides us and teaches us. HE carries our burden. HE is our strength. We get to just rest in Him while all our needs are being provided for.

Regarding authority, we can walk in spiritual authority from either tree. So, just because you can do something in your own strength, doesn't make it "right" or "good." Anytime we operate from our own strength, there will still be death woven into it EVEN if it's a "good" thing you are doing. Furthermore, it is even possible to correctly discern or judge something from the Tree of Knowledge...BUT since the Tree of Knowledge was used, now the correct judgment will fall short because it is not rooted in life (the Tree of Life)! The correct judgment was perverted because it was attained through striving instead of oneness. My judgment of the high-profile Christian leader I mentioned earlier in the book is a GREAT example of this. My judgment of him *was* accurate, BUT I was not operating from the Tree of Life, so I was in error. Anything done outside of love will have death in it.

Doing ANYTHING while disconnected from Yahweh, even if you are trying to do it FOR Yahweh, brings death because we rejected the oneness within us by doing something on our own and out of our pea-brain understanding. Our ignorance of spiritual (or even natural) things does not affect their reality. We are still affected by the spiritual and natural laws around us regardless of our awareness or ignorance. A child's ignorance of gravity does not prevent them from falling on their face. Similarly, our ignorance of the Tree of Knowledge does not change the death we bring into situations, even our ministries!

On a quick note, I do want to clarify that knowledge itself is not *inherently* bad. Remember that one of the seven spirits of God is the spirit of KNOWLEDGE (Isaiah 11:2). We have a GOOD Father who WANTS us to grow and mature. In James 14:26, it even says that Holy Spirit will teach you ALL things. Knowledge was not the sin, it was rejecting and disobeying God that brought Adam and Eve death. So now we are on a journey of renewing our mind and learning how to do life WITH Father God after generations (and generations!) of operating from the Tree of Knowledge. We were pursuing knowledge through the Tree of Knowledge, but ALL knowledge is found in the Tree of Life! Knowledge was never the issue, it has always come down to what tree we operated from.

The journey of untangling from the Tree of Knowledge begins as we explore and embrace ONENESS. All we have known was how to weigh, measure, and judge life through what we *think* we know. These judgments and separations of "good" and "evil" are a form of polarization. In our blindness and ignorance, we are constantly measuring and polarizing our lives. Light is good, and darkness is bad. Rest is good, and stress is bad. This food is good, and that food is bad. This political party/ideology is good, and that one is bad. The list goes on and on and on. The polarizing and judging are what EVERYONE does, so it is very foreign just to consider the concept of life without polarizing and judging.

Furthermore, when we polarize/live from the Tree of Knowledge, we invest emotion into a judgment of someone or something, and then we are bound to what we polarized through our emotion and judgment! For example, when I judged the high-profile Christian leader, I was BOUND by my judgment and blinded to seeing Yahweh's heart for him. The weighing and judging in our own strength brings death AND binds us to the very things we polarized. So, the first step to untangling from the Tree of Knowledge is to ENGAGE with Jesus and SURRENDER the areas that you think you "know." Sounds familiar, doesn't it? EVERYTHING, absolutely EVERYTHING, comes back to our ONENESS with Jesus! You can NOT untangle from the Tree of Knowledge in your own strength. As we break agreement with and surrender our polarization, we free our soul to hear TRUTH because we are no longer bound to what we thought we knew.

Jesus (the Tree of Life) IS the vine, and we are the branches. Everything comes back to our connection to the source. Yahweh, Jesus, and Holy Spirit are faithful to us. They have paid the highest price for us to have access to the Tree of Life, and they are more invested in our choosing life than we are. To start untangling from the Tree of Knowledge, simply start asking Jesus (or Holy Spirit or Yahweh) about it!

As we choose the Tree of Life and embrace it for ourselves, then God will begin to teach us HOW to do everything with Him/in Life. The old dogma, boxes, and striving that we operated from fade away, and a subtle (but powerful) stillness, anchoring, and empowerment take their place! In the Tree of Life, there is a balance, oneness, and centeredness that becomes the foundation of your life, actions, and perspective. You will begin to see abundant life and learn to operate from it. (You will also begin to see the goodness of God in EVERYTHING, masterfully woven into even the most horrific of circumstances. To a hurting and blind soul, that is a VERY offensive statement, but if you will push past the offense, you will find wholeness and goodness like you never thought possible!)

To see the bigger picture, it helps to take a step back and evaluate what Yahweh and Jesus did in the Bible. God is THE example of balance and oneness. And as we explore what life looks like from Heaven's perspective (the Tree of Life), we begin to see that the Bible, creation, and the gospel are pictures of ONENESS. In the beginning, Yahweh created light AND dark, and He said it was GOOD. He created the positive and negative magnetic fields that literally sustain creation. He created opposing elements like fire and water. He is a God of mercy and judgment. All throughout creation, we see examples of opposing concepts working together in God's GOOD plan. In Jesus' life, we know that He never sinned which means He solely lived from the Tree of Life. During His time on earth, Jesus fasted, and He feasted. He was joyful, and He wept. He healed people, and He flipped tables. Jesus withdrew from people, and He went to the crowds. He worked long hours, and He also took naps. He encouraged, and He rebuked. He danced, and He mourned. He abided by "religious protocol" at times, and other times He blew EVERYONE out of the water. In Yahweh and Jesus' actions, we can see there are lots of seemingly opposing concepts or actions that all fall under the umbrella of God's GOODness and good plan.

God's ways and perspectives are VERY different from man's ways. For example, just look at Jesus' FIRST recorded miracle... turning water into wine for people who were already drunk! We DEFINITELY would have judged that as "bad!" Another fun example...I can just about guarantee that if Jesus HIMSELF hadn't flipped the tables, we would have called that behavior "bad." This goes to show that OUR judgment of good and evil is VERY different from Yahweh's. If our version of "good" and "bad" clashes with God's perspective, then we have a LOT of untangling and renewing that needs to happen in order for us to start learning how to live from the Tree of Life. Basically, living from the Tree of Life looks VERY different than what our idea of living from the Tree of Life would look like.

In the Garden of Eden, there was no "law" to worry about. There was no *knowledge* of "good" and "evil" for Adam and Eve to judge and live by. Life in the garden boiled down to two things... abundant life and the choice/ability to reject God. THIS model (free from the law) was GOOD in God's eyes. It is how HE set up the garden! As we untangle from the Tree of Knowledge, we find that we no longer polarize and measure life. In the Tree of Life, there is only...LIFE. The striving ceases because we aren't trying to do things in our own strength. We have CONFIDENCE in the GOODNESS of Yahweh. We no longer fear that God is holding out on us, and we know where we stand with Him. We do EVERYTHING from oneness and bliss, because no matter what, there is LIFE in everything.

There is a LOT for us to surrender and let go of just to begin to grasp the concepts of the Tree of Life. EVERYTHING in our old nature REJECTS the Tree of Life. Because of sin, it is practically hardwired into our flesh to reject God and His nature. BUT as we explore the Tree of Life and allow Jesus to speak into our lives in this way, EVERYTHING changes. Our perspective, our life source, our thoughts, and our actions are all radically transformed in the Tree of Life. And it all starts so simply...by engaging and agreeing with the oneness we have with Jesus who is already within us!

PAIN AND THE TREE OF LIFE

Probably my biggest block to living from the Tree of Life was my fear of pain (for myself and others). I was not ok with pain and therefore was not ok with others being in pain. I believed that discomfort, suffering, and pain should be avoided. Even my motivation for doing ministry was to help others avoid or reduce their pain. It was a MASSIVE idol (focus) in my heart, and I spent many years talking with Jesus before I chose to align myself with His perspective. Once I got past the hurdle of the fear of pain, I felt the blinders come off my eyes. We are predominantly pain-motivated beings. For the first time ever, I was able to see that 99.9999% of the time, we live and plan our lives around pain.

I'll explain. We pick our careers and live our lives around what will bring us our desired level of comfort. Either we push ourselves hard to make more money...so we can be comfortable. Or we pick easy jobs that don't push us hard...to be comfortable. And *sometimes* people pick jobs to reduce other people's pain... to make *them* more comfortable. Physical health is another example of us making choices based on our desired level of comfort. Someone may work out (which isn't comfortable), but they work out so that either they can defend themselves or their family (which reduces pain), OR so that they are healthier (which reduces the pain of the body falling apart later in life). Even doing things out of religious duty...is done to make things more "comfortable" for us (less painful) when we "die and go to Heaven."

The more I got free from the fear of pain, the more I realized that we are constantly thinking about how to avoid pain in our lives or the lives of others. We live in reaction to pain and suffering and try to find the path of the least pain. This also means that our soul's version of "compassion" is merely a knee-jerk reaction to someone else's pain because it is rooted in fear and self-protection. Whereas kingdom compassion is GROWTH-motivated, not pain motivated. True kindness and compassion look through the eyes of love and from an eternal, big-picture perspective.

Fear of pain blocks us from seeing the GOODNESS of God in the world around us, stunts our soul growth, and keeps us in torment (because we are in agreement with fear). I discuss how to address fear in depth in Chapter 2 of Book 3 (BEcoming Whole), but summarized, dealing with fear is the same process as dealing with any other lie: identify the lie, break agreement with it, and receive what Jesus has to say in its place. ANY time we agree with a lie of the enemy, we are rejecting Jesus (the Tree of Life) and are striving in our own strength to attain something (which is operating from the Tree of Knowledge). In regard to my fear of pain, I didn't like what Jesus told me. I wanted to stay in my delusion because I didn't like the true reality Jesus was showing me.

Once I came to terms with what Jesus was showing me, my soul was freed to be able to start seeing the bigger picture. Pain is inevitable in this life, and fearing pain only brings MORE pain to us. We live in a broken world, but we can take heart because JESUS has taken the sting out of every pain and death. God outdoes Himself with the extravagant goodness and redemption He lavishes on EVERY single pain. God does not WANT us to be in pain (remember the model of the garden). He is a GOOD Father who wants a GOOD life for His kids. But He also is not afraid of pain and suffering...He promises to bring good from ALL things. He takes what the enemy meant to destroy us and uses the pain as a tool for our breakthrough.

While learning how to live free from pain motivation (fear of pain), I learned that God is more concerned with our growth than our comfort. The Tree of Life/God's nature is NEVER motivated by fear or pain. Fear does not exist in the Tree of Life perspective. There is only LIFE. So if we do experience pain, we can see the JOY set before us and endure whatever we are facing. From the Tree of Life perspective, our suffering is not worth comparing to the beauty and glory God brings from our pain!

PAIN AND DISCIPLINE

Nobody likes pain. Period. But as a parent, now I have a totally different perspective on the discomfort of discipline. I don't *want* to discipline my children, but I do because I know that it's in their best interest. If I don't discipline my children, I set them up for failure and dysfunction in life! The same principle applies to our walk. We are reborn, babies in Christ, and we have a

GOOD Father...actually the best! He is incredibly intentional and wholeheartedly invested in us. I also believe that the Father is as gentle as possible, but as firm as necessary, with us. Check out this verse...

> Hebrews 12:5-11 (TPT) "And have you forgotten his encouraging words spoken to you as his children? He said, "My child, don't underestimate the value of the discipline and training of the Lord God, or get depressed when he has to correct you. _For the Lord's training of your life is the evidence of his faithful love. And when he draws you to himself, it proves you are his delightful child._" Fully embrace God's correction as part of your training, for he is doing what any loving father does for his children. For who has ever heard of a child who never had to be corrected? _We all should welcome God's discipline as the validation of authentic sonship._ For if we have never once endured his correction it only proves we are strangers and not sons. And isn't it true that we respect our earthly fathers even though they corrected and disciplined us? Then we should demonstrate an even greater respect for God, our spiritual Father, as we submit to his life-giving discipline. Our parents corrected us for the short time of our childhood as it seemed good to them. _But God corrects us throughout our lives for our own good, giving us an invitation to share his holiness. Now all discipline seems to be painful at the time, yet later it will produce a transformation of character, bringing a harvest of righteousness and peace to those who yield to it._" [Emphasis mine]

"The Lord's training is EVIDENCE of his faithful love...God corrects us throughout our lives for OUR own good, giving us an invitation to share in his holiness...it will produce a TRANSFORMATION of character, bringing a harvest of righteousness and peace to those who YIELD to it." What a

POWERFUL section of scripture! As we begin to see scripture through the eyes of a loving parent, we begin to see a very different picture.

Yahweh ALLOWED the Israelites to be conquered multiple times when their hearts became hardened. Their discomfort was not as important as their hearts turning back to Him. If we refuse to soften our hearts towards Yahweh, He will allow/use external circumstances to cause enough discomfort to encourage us to choose life instead of death. Our actions and circumstances are fleeting and but a vapor, so they don't matter as much as our heart does. Please hear me clearly, God is NOT sadistic and out to make His kids' lives terrible. We NEVER see that example in scripture. It is His KINDNESS that leads us to repentance (Romans 2:4). God does EVERYTHING in love, and His ministry is the ministry of reconciliation. He loves us too much to leave us in our brokenness, and this is why God is growth motivated instead of pain motivated.

As a parent, nothing brings me more joy than seeing my children enjoy the good times and good things I give them. At the same time, nothing makes me prouder than to see my children grow and stand firm in hard times. I don't *want* the hard times for them, but I see the value and beauty of the hard times because of the character it grows. I want my children to grow into mature and powerful sons of God. When parenting my children, I will discipline and counsel my children so that they grow. I know that their character and walk with God is the most important thing I can help them grow in, so it trumps my desire to make life easy and perfect for them. And we see God doing the same thing with us. Remember that God LEFT the giants in the Promised Land for the Israelites to learn how to fight...

> Judges 3:1-2 (NLT) "These are the nations that the LORD left in the land to test those Israelites who had not experienced the wars of Canaan. He did this to teach warfare to generations of Israelites who had no experience in battle."

God didn't leave giants in the land to make his kids suffer...He left the giants FOR them! At some point, they realized that God was allowing the giants for THEIR benefit...

> *Numbers 14:9 (BSB) "Only do not rebel against the LORD, and do not be afraid of the people of the land, <u>for they will be like bread for us</u>. Their protection has been removed, and the LORD is with us. Do not be afraid of them!" [Emphasis mine]*

God knew that conquering giants was NOURISHMENT for their soul! Many of our lives would look very different if we viewed the giants of our life as BREAD for us. If we stand firm, we will see the faithfulness of God in ways we never thought possible. Remember that it is Yahweh who prepares the FEAST in the presence of our enemies. The choice is ours if we will come and sit at His table or turn away in fear or offense.

In times when the Israelites hardened their heart against God, <u>Yahweh allowed them to be conquered to bring them back to Him.</u> It was better to let them reap what they were sowing SO THAT they would turn back to Him than to leave them with hardened hearts.

> *Psalms 119:67 (NLT) "I used to wander off until you disciplined me; but now I closely follow your word."*

> *Isaiah 48:10 (NLT) "I have refined you, but not as silver is refined. Rather, I have refined you in the furnace of suffering."*

> *Psalms 119:71-72 (NLT) "My suffering was good for me, for it taught me to pay attention to your decrees. Your instructions are more valuable to me than millions in gold and silver."*

> *Job 36:16-17 (NLT) "<u>God is leading you away from danger</u>, Job, to a place free from distress. <u>He is</u>*

setting your table with the best food. But you are *obsessed with whether the godless will be judged.* *Don't worry, judgment and justice will be upheld.* *Be on guard! Turn back from evil, for God sent* *this suffering to keep you from a life of evil."* *[Emphasis mine]*

Job 36:15 (NLT) "But by means of their suffering, *he rescues those who suffer. For he gets their* *attention through adversity."*

I especially love those verses in Job. Job wasn't getting picked on by God. God was leading Job AWAY from danger to keep him FROM a life of evil. The Lord disciplines those He loves. It is better to allow adversity to soften the hearts of His children than to leave us hard against Him. Is all suffering sent from God because we had a hard heart? NO. In this life, we are guaranteed hard times regardless of our heart posture. (Just look at Jesus' life!)

QUICK BUT IMPORTANT NOTE: Remember that *the enemy always creates polar-opposite lies to* *deceive us from the truth. Just because God is* *growth motivated, does NOT mean we should* *cause as much pain as possible in our own life* *to help ourselves grow. That is a sadistic and* *demonic suggestion. For us to try to cause* *hardship and suffering so we can "grow" ourselves* *COMPLETELY misses the point. We would be* *right back at square one, trying to decide with* *the Tree of Knowledge, what would be "enough"* *hardship to "grow" us. In doing that, we would be* *using the Tree of Knowledge and bringing DEATH* *into our life and circumstances. There is NO life* *that comes from self-persecution. Jesus didn't go* *out of His way to make His life hard. He is our* *example; God in the flesh. And we don't see any* *self-persecution actions or teachings in Jesus'* *life. All this to say, we can disregard any thoughts to make our life harder through some twisted self-persecution to grow more into our own self-created ideas.*

Sons of God don't fear pain (or self-inflict pain) because we live from the Tree of Life and see pain from a Heavenly perspective. When pain comes, it can be used to MAKE us, not break us. There is nothing to fear...EVER. The more we operate from the Tree of Life, the more we will be convinced of the goodness of God and live from Heaven's perspective. Below is an excerpt from BEcoming Whole (*Book 3*) where I tried to explain how hard times and suffering look VERY different through the eyes of Heaven. For context, I had this vision right after I lost three friends slowly and painfully to cancer...

> *In the vision, Jesus brought me one of my friends who had just died. I was SHOCKED to see her. She was so young, healthy, whole in the soul, and GLOWING! She looked GREAT! I shouted out, "Kerry!! Oh my goodness! It is so good to see you! I am SO sorry I couldn't heal you or raise you from the dead. I tried my best." Kerry was glowing and smiling the biggest smile I have ever seen. She said to me, "Jessica, it is FINE! It was nothing."*
>
> *"NOTHING", she said??? I saw her die. I saw Kerry slowly and painfully wither away from surgery after surgery and treatment after treatment. I saw Kerry's spouse slowly die of cancer earlier. I didn't understand, so I asked, "NOTHING? How can you say that was nothing? That was a terribly painful and horrible way to die." Kerry, unfazed and still glowing answered, "Jessica, all I see is Jesus when I look back at my time on earth. I don't see or feel the pain. From Heaven's perspective, I can truly say it was nothing." I had a small grid for what Kerry was talking about. My memories of sexual abuse have been re-written by Jesus. When I look back at my memories now, all I see is*

Jesus, and all I feel is His peace. There is no more pain or trauma. Jesus has healed those moments in my life. So when Kerry told me that all she sees is Jesus, I had a grid for understanding what she was talking about. If Jesus could do it for my traumatic memories, of course, He could do it for Kerry's whole life. Then I remembered Kerry's kids. Now they have lost BOTH parents to cancer in a short amount of time. So I asked Kerry about her kids. Her answer blew me away even more...

Kerry smiled even bigger than before (which just made her glow more) and said, "Jessica, my kids are going to be just fine! There is no fear in this realm. Jesus is so big and so good. My kids are in GOOD hands. Everything will work out for good." When Kerry said that, I instantly knew that that didn't mean her kids wouldn't face hardships. Kerry had an unshakable confidence and peace in Yahweh. Jesus was good to Kerry's kids and loved them even more than Kerry did. So even in a broken world, her kids were in good hands. And if they didn't get healed on that side, they were going to experience the same healing and breakthrough that both their parents did on the other side. Everything would be fine and made new.

This encounter was a marked moment in my life. I saw another facet of the goodness of God. Once again, Jesus blew me away with His wonderfulness. Everything really was going to be ok, even in this painful and broken world. Healing IS available to our earthly bodies, but if we don't get healed physically, then Jesus is STILL good and big enough to redeem it all. Either way, everything will be just fine. There will be pain in this world, but it will not last...nor will we even consider it! (Romans 8:18) Being free from the fear of pain changes everything.

In the Tree of Life, I am learning how to be carefree. When we cast our cares on Jesus, we become free from care. It does not mean that we are careless, it just means that we are no longer the ones carrying our cares. JESUS carries the weight of the world. HE carries my cares and my emotions...and in return... my burden IS light! I never understood that verse while I was in religion. There was nothing "light" about religion! In the Tree of Life, I am truly free. This life is a vapor, and I am convinced of the goodness of God even in the midst of suffering. We can't lose!

Please remember that all of this download came from sitting with Jesus. We can't learn or think our way out of the Tree of Knowledge. We can't do it. We never could do it. Our flesh REJECTS God and His ways. So I encourage you to explore this WITH Jesus. As you surrender what you think you "know" and break agreement with any fear of pain, you will begin the journey of untangling from the Tree of Knowledge. Your burden will be light, your cares will be lifted, and you will be overwhelmed with the GOODNESS of God!

The Tree of Life really is all about ONENESS. We are called to be continually connected to the vine, not just in times of need or crisis. It would be ridiculous for someone to take one breath and expect that one breath to sustain them all day...or all week! Yet that is how we treat our relationship with God. We expect one prayer time to last us all day or even all week when it was never intended to be like that. We are ONE with Christ. Separation is impossible. Living from the Tree of Life boils down to our whole being continually living from oneness. That's all it is.

The gospel is simple, and the Tree of Life is simple. Abide in Him! Our yoke actually IS easy, and our burden is light. HE fills the cup. HE prepares the table. HE works all things out for good. The thing Yahweh doesn't do for us is...eliminate our free will. To preserve our freedom, we are responsible for our soul. We couldn't do it alone. So Yahweh, in His brilliance, empowered us by making us ONE spirit with Christ. So one part of us, our spirit, is empowered to do ANYTHING in Christ, nothing is impossible for us now. And the same time, Yahweh preserved our free will in our soul so that we could still choose to reject God if we wanted to. Our responsibility is to renew all the real estate of our mind by engaging our free will to choose Yahweh in every area. As we choose Yahweh in every area, more and more of our soul will be connected to and living from the Tree of Life. Our burden is light, and our cup is overflowing. There is LIFE in everything we do because we are one with, and living from, abundant Life Himself.

Chapter Nine

FINALLY A CHAPTER ON DOING

It only took me four books to finally talk about DOING! (*I hope you have gotten the hint that our actions are not as important as our heart.*) Jesus spent 30 YEARS walking in intimacy with Yahweh BEFORE He started His ministry. Sooooo...I don't feel bad about taking this long to talk about doing. Let's start with this precious conversation...

> *John 6:28-29 (NLT) "They replied, 'We want to perform God's works, too. What should we do?' Jesus told them, 'This is the only work God wants from you: Believe in the one he has sent.'"* [Emphasis mine]

Jesus' answer to His disciples was not a list of actions. Instead, it was "RECEIVE ME." First we receive, then we do. *But what about all the commands like heal the sick, raise the dead, cast our demons, preach the good news, and care for the widows and orphans?* WHY didn't Jesus say any of these? Because these COmmands are examples of what a son of God LOOKS like. These things OVERFLOW naturally out of our being, without striving!

Because our actions flow out from the abundance of our HEART... God really DOES care more about our heart than our actions! If our heart is abundantly broken, our actions will be out of brokenness. (Even "good" actions done from a place of brokenness are ROOTED in death.) If our heart is walking in abundant LIFE, then our actions will be filled with life. Bill

Johnson puts it beautifully, "Love God with all your heart and do whatever you want." If we truly love God with all our heart, then we will be like Him and bring LIFE into all that we do.

So that's it. As you believe in Jesus, your life will be transformed, including your actions. Do you want to be an actor? GREAT! God is needed there! Do you want to be a teacher? GREAT! God is needed there! Do you want to be a stay-at-home mom? GREAT! God is needed there! Whatever you choose to do, you will find yourself healing the sick, casting out demons, preaching the good news, and so on. You become the embodiment of the gospel on the earth as you enter His rest. Without trying, you will be the hands and feet of Love on the earth!

So don't worry about doing. The doing will come from the abundance of your heart. Believe in (receive) the one He has sent, and the rest will follow. It is simple. HE will father you in all things, even doing. God intentionally doesn't give us formulas, so to DO His things, we must live from the oneness we have with Him. Below is our life mantra, the foundation of the gospel, the overflow of our heart. EVERYTHING in our life starts here...

"The Father and I are one."

Chapter Ten

FINDING JOY

For many years now, I have been living satisfied, at rest, and content in Jesus. It wasn't until recently that a question/ realization "dropped" into my soul... *"Where is the joy?"* (I'm sure Jesus planted the question for me to discover and explore!) I had found peace, contentment, and healing in Jesus, but I noticed my joy was lacking. The Bible mentions "joy overflowing" and "the joy of the Lord being our strength," but those concepts felt foreign to me. I never prioritized joy because "life isn't about being happy." I sought after Jesus for my sustenance, for my peace, for my healing... and I found all of them in abundance! But I had never pursued joy.

As I pondered joy, I softened my heart to be able to receive revelation on it. That is when Jesus showed me just a glimpse of joy. In that glimpse, I saw that it was a VALUABLE part of Yahweh, and that it WAS worth pursuing! From that moment on, I wanted to chase after joy. I realized for the first time that life isn't about being "happy," BUT the joy of the Lord is part of MY inheritance. It is part of the fabric of Heaven and part of who Jesus is! I decided that if I was going to seek after joy, I wanted the real deal instead of some cheap counterfeit. In the world, happiness is fleeting. Even in the church, most of the "joy" we see seems to be a mask that is only put on for occasions. I was not interested in a fleeting moment of joy. I have gotten whacked with joy at a conference here and there. It was fun to "play in the water," but it was not lasting. Instead of just a visitation, I set my heart to find a habitation of joy. I set my heart to BECOME joy. I knew deep in my soul that lasting joy could become as unshakable as my peace and confidence in Yahweh. I was also very excited to pursue joy because I knew Jesus gave me the desire for joy SO THAT I could find it.

> *1 Chronicles 16:27 (ESV) "Splendor and majesty are before him; strength and joy are in his place."* [Emphasis mine]

> *Romans 14:17 (TPT) "For the kingdom of God is not a matter of rules about food and drink, but is in the realm of the Holy Spirit, filled with righteousness, peace, and joy."* [Emphasis mine]

> *Acts 2:28 (NLT) "You have shown me the way of life, and you will fill me with the joy of your presence."* [Emphasis mine]

> *John 15:11 (NLT) "I have told you these things so that you will be filled with my joy. Yes, your joy will overflow."* [Emphasis mine]

> *Psalms 30:11 (NLT) "You have turned my mourning into joyful dancing. You have taken away my clothes of mourning and clothed me with joy."*

Even when I was in religion, I believed that Yahweh was a God of JOY. He created a garden and named it "pleasure." He COMMANDED the Israelites to party (have festivals) multiple times a year. HE spreads the table for us. HE fills our cup to overflowing. In HIM is fullness of joy. HIS joy is our strength. And it was for the JOY that was set before Jesus that He endured the cross. In religion, I could see the *existence* of these things Biblically, but this kind of joy felt FOREIGN to my soul. Sooooo, like everything else, I asked Jesus about it! I thought I would engage Jesus, meet the being of joy, and go on a wild encounter that would push me out of my comfort zone. Instead, Jesus revealed that there were lies I was believing (more soul beliefs) that were rejecting joy. If I were to try to engage with joy, my soul would resist it! And I would make little to no progress in finding joy until these lies were addressed.

When I began to ask Jesus about joy, He told me to first address the "downcast parts" of my soul. These disheartened areas were not only affecting my joy, but they were blocking my ability to even receive revelation on joy. After meditating and engaging Jesus about these "downcast parts," I was able to see that they were simply the areas of my heart that were still fixated on earthly troubles. What our soul fixates on, we become. This is why God tells us to fix our eyes on <u>heavenly</u> things. If our soul is fixated on earthly things, then our soul will take on wrong ideologies and operate as if it were a citizen of earth.

Quick note: You may be wondering about the term "soul parts." Our soul is a highly sophisticated operating system that is the control center for our body and spirit. Part of its sophistication is the soul's ability to keep operating in spite of experiencing incredible pain, disillusionment, and trauma. When the soul doesn't know how to address something painful, it will break the painful part off and then stash that soul part somewhere "out of sight." (Kind of like how a wild animal will chew off its own limb if the limb becomes stuck in a trap...only the soul can't escape the chewed-off limb, it still carries its weight) By stuffing the pain, the soul is able to dysfunctionally pretend that there has been resolve and keep on living. "Out of sight" in soul terms just means they are now subconscious! They are still there, but we are unaware of them. Stuffing soul parts may keep you "functioning" (dysfunctionally), but those broken soul parts add more weight that we have to carry even though they are "out of sight." It is exhausting, AND our soul can't prevent those broken parts from being triggered. Since they were not actually healed, those hidden soul parts can become triggered at any point. For example, if a movie, a conversation, or a similar event, reminds your soul of the buried pain...then the hidden soul parts will unstuff themselves, get on their soap box, and proclaim their brokenness. This is why someone can be totally fine one moment, and then totally not ok the next. The more unaddressed soul parts we have, the greater the reaction our soul will manifest.

When Jesus highlighted the "downcast parts of my soul," He was revealing areas of pain that I had stuffed. I did not realize that there were MANY parts of my soul that were still fixated on earthly things. I have spent years with Jesus healing the deeply traumatized parts of my soul that were screaming in pain. Once I dealt with the "big ones," I thought I was good to go, but there were still many parts that lingered quietly in pain and dysfunction ...they just weren't screaming! These downcast parts took root before I learned how to bring things to Jesus, so they remained unhealed and out of sight until they became triggered or highlighted by Jesus. (Thank you Jesus for bringing them to my attention!)

I asked Jesus how to heal these downcast parts of my soul, and one by one reconciled each one back to Jesus. I am intentionally omitting the process Jesus took me through to address the downcast parts of my soul. This process was specific to me and not a formula. If you feel that you have downcast parts of your soul blocking your joy, then ask Jesus about it. He is the source and will show you how to heal your soul.

Dealing with the downcast parts of my soul was like peeling an onion. Once those soul parts were reconciled, I was able to see the next layer of soul dysfunction that was affecting my agreement/reception of joy. To my surprise, I had unknowingly made multiple judgments AGAINST joy! My soul was bound by my judgment and rejection of joy, and until I addressed it, my joy would remain throttled. Some of these may sound familiar to you and some of these may just be a me-thing, but I listed them all to help expose some of the lies we believe about joy...

1. I thought joy wasn't a priority because "life isn't about being happy."

    I never realized that religion built its gospel around a grumpy God and sinful man. The law (legalism) brings wrath, so religion needed to find a way to justify its own wrath (grumpy attitude). To validate its grumpy gospel (serve, grovel, strive, and slave till you die), we were told religiously that "life isn't about being happy." In reality, we are ONE spirit with a joy-filled God who laughs and dances.

The pursuit of happiness is meaningless, BUT we find joy and pleasure evermore as we pursue Yahweh Himself. There is no grumpy gospel in Heaven...there is no grumpiness in Heaven! There IS an abundance of LOVE, JOY, and PEACE everywhere!

2. I thought joy was wild and emotional (which meant that it would be unstable and inconsistent). I thought it was better to be "anchored," and "anchored" looked like stability and consistency. To be wild was "childlike," and the mature were "steady."

    Religion shows a picture of the wise being very stoic. The weight of maturity and responsibility is "serious stuff." That may be how religion paints it, but David was praised for his undignified dancing and wildness. He was a man after God's heart. When we look at Jesus, we don't see a stoic and "consistent" example. Instead, Jesus went to weddings, celebrated feasts, and told the disciples that He desired them to have His overflowing joy (John 15:11). Jesus was unpredictable and passionate; and yet He was anchored, wise, and mature. Paul also mentions in the Bible that there would be times of ecstasy and pure bliss that we could be caught up in. If we want to embrace God for all of who He is, joy will be part of that.

    2 Corinthians 5:13 (TPT) "If we are out of our minds in a blissful, divine ecstasy, it is for God, but if we are in our right minds, it is for your benefit."

3. I thought joy was the least valuable of the fruits of the Holy Spirit. *(In church, I was taught to strive to be loving, patient, kind, and self-controlled. But because "life isn't about being happy," church never honored joy.)*

    It's not "the peace of the Lord" or "the self-control of the Lord" that is our strength. It's the JOY of the Lord! Religion has massively downplayed joy, but JOY is a strategic gift from Yahweh!

Nehemiah 8:10b (NLT) "...Don't be dejected and sad, <u>for the</u> <u>joy of the Lord is your strength!</u>" [Emphasis mine]

I *thought* I had untangled from religion...but I still had some very religious mindsets regarding joy! (I am sure there is much more that I am blind to; I am still in process.) YAY God for freedom!! Jesus was so kind to first drop the question, *"Where is my joy?"*, in my heart and then reveal to me the parts of my soul that needed renewing SO THAT I could receive His gift of joy! After dealing with the downcast parts of my soul and repenting from the judgments I made, I still didn't have a wild encounter with the being of joy. Instead, I had a "duh" moment while I was pondering joy with Jesus. Joy was not something I would "find" in a moment, it would be something I would grow in, just like peace. In Jesus, I have found peace that surpasses understanding and circumstance. I didn't "find" peace in a single moment. It has been years of cultivating peace, chasing after it, and meditating on how to stay in peace no matter my circumstances. It was such a "duh" moment for me when I realized that joy is something we grow in and cultivate over time and with Jesus (just like everything else in our walk!).

It took me hours of sitting with Jesus just to soften my soul enough to receive understanding on the downcast parts of my soul. As my history with God grows, more and more real estate of my soul will be renewed and anchored in His joy. In my process of pursuing joy, it dawned on me that it would be good to ask Jesus WHAT the joy of the Lord even was! I always thought of joy as a deeper, more lasting form of happiness. To my surprise, this is the definition I heard from Jesus:

"The Joy of the Lord is delighting in the goodness of God."

I wasn't expecting that answer, but my soul drank it up! *"Delighting in the goodness of God."* YES! OF COURSE! As I meditated on that definition, I could see the power of focusing on the goodness of God. Anytime we focus on GOOD things, our spirits are lifted and become more and more DELIGHTED! Yahweh delights in His Son, and He delights in us. When we then choose to delight in Yahweh, we synergize with the joy of the Lord, and it becomes our strength.

Joy is a choice...that can also be accompanied by an emotion. Sometimes the emotion is or is not there, but that doesn't have to affect my choice to choose joy. I choose to love my husband regardless of whether I *feel* the emotion of love towards him or not. In the same way, I can choose joy regardless of my circumstances. It's not something that happens to me, it's a choice. [#mindblown]

CULTIVATING JOY

Instead of "finding" joy, we have ALREADY been given joy because we are ONE spirit with Jesus. It is simply a matter of our soul CHOOSING to not reject the joy that is already in us. We can cultivate it and grow our soul's capacity to walk in agreement with the joy of the Lord. If joy is a choice, then we are the ones responsible to engage our free will to pursue joy and address the unrenewed areas of our heart. BESIDES asking Jesus about joy, here are a couple of practical things you can do to cultivate it...

- Break agreement with any judgments you have made against joy.

- CHOOSE to celebrate, dance, and look at the GOOD that is around you.

  o Whatever you fixate on, you become. So FIX your eyes on heavenly things, like the goodness of God and His GREAT plan to win big!

- Prioritize time in your day to laugh

  o Laughter is good medicine. It heals your body and pulls your soul up. What makes you laugh? Your favorite comedian? Jokes? Funny cat videos? You can ask Jesus for a strategy on how to make yourself laugh. For those with really downcast souls, it may be helpful to fake laugh just to remind your soul how to laugh.

If we want to grow in something, we have to exercise ourselves in that thing. For example, if you want to grow your muscles, you exercise your muscles. If you want to grow in joy, you practice joy. Please understand that when you intentionally choose to practice joy, it is not being fake. Wearing a mask of joy is different from practicing joy. A mask is put on for other people, whereas practicing joy is training your soul to grow its capacity. Remember that the reason WHY you do something is the important part! You can choose to laugh so people think you are happy, or you can choose to laugh to train your soul to choose joy!

As you grow your capacity to walk in joy, you will find that joy is more than just happy feelings. Joy IS joyful, but it is ALSO:

- A technology that softens pain
  - *Hebrews 12:2 (BSB) "Let us fix our eyes on Jesus, the author and perfector of our faith, who for the joy set before Him endured the cross, scorning its shame, and sat down at the right hand of the throne of God."*

- Strength in the face of uncertainty
  - *Nehemiah 8:10b (NLT) "...Don't be dejected and sad, for the joy of the Lord is your strength!"*

- Literally healing to our soul and body
  - *Proverbs 17:22 (ESV) "A joyful heart is good medicine, but a crushed spirit dries up the bones."*

The benefits of joy are deep and wide. The deeper you explore joy, the more you will become it. Remember that Yahweh is INCREDIBLY intentional with everything He does. Not only did HE create joy, but He also put healing, strength, and even courage into the DNA of joy. Joy IS worth pursuing!

WILD JOY

> *Psalms 16:11 (NLT) "You will show me the way of life, granting me the joy of your presence and the pleasures of living with you forever." [Emphasis mine]*

By now you may be open to and even desiring to go after joy... but what about wild joy? Wild joy goes deeper than delight. It's an overwhelming force that brings our soul into a state of ecstasy and bliss as we engage Yahweh without restraint. Wild joy goes beyond our wildest dreams. It is the realm of pleasures forever more. It is something we can get caught up in outside of time and space (our circumstances). It is a state of not being able to tell where you end and Yahweh begins. The joy of the Lord can be ever present in our lives, and then there are times when this "blissful, divine ecstasy" is available to us...

> *2 Corinthians 5:13 (TPT) "If we are out of our minds in a blissful, divine ecstasy, it is for God, but if we are in our right minds, it is for your benefit."*

Instead of using "blissful, divine ecstasy," many of the other translations say "beside myself" for this Greek word *"existēmi."* *Existēmi* means: to be out of one's mind, beside yourself, or insane! Normally it would sound really bad to be insane or out of our mind (notice the judgment there from the Tree of Knowledge?), BUT we are literally called to put on the mind of Christ! And the mind of Christ will ALWAYS *look* insane to an unrenewed mind operating in the world's systems. (If you have any religious mindsets left regarding joy...they are the ones squirming right now.)

This wild joy of bliss and ecstasy is ALREADY within you. It is part of Heaven which means it's another facet of Yahweh. Wild joy will naturally flow out from us as our soul heals, and we stop shaming and rejecting this blissful, divine ecstasy. Will our lives always be wild and in a state of ecstasy? No. Will it be at times?

Yes...IF we don't throttle it! There are times and seasons for everything even with Yahweh. For example, there are times of joy and bliss, times of intense heaviness and weight, and times of rest and healing. Blissful, divine ecstasy is just another facet available to us within the scope of our relationship with Yahweh.

Interestingly, I have found this radical joy to be very appealing to non-religious people. For obvious reasons, it sounds like a WONDERFUL time (without having to use drugs or alcohol)! But for those who were raised in religion, this wild joy is HIGHLY concerning....because religion is all about CONTROL. (annnnd there it is!) I was shocked that my soul was squirming at the idea of being "out of my mind" in wild joy...until I realized that it was rooted in religion and control! To be wildly joyful looked wildly out of control and unstable. Even as a mom or when I was a kid's pastor, I would be "wild" and full of energy, BUT I was always still in control. I rejected any invitations from Yahweh to be out of my mind in blissful, divine ecstasy so that I could stay in control. Now I was being confronted with actually being out of control in regards to wild joy...and it was deeply unnerving for me.

Religion paints a picture where the "holiness" of God is a stoic and serious presence. So the closer you get to "holiness" (maturing in God) the more serious and solemn you become. The religious spirit is sneaky and weaves its lies and perspectives into everything. Up till this point in my life, I thought I knew what maturity was. Then in a moment, it all came crashing down. I could see that I had a self-created idea of what maturity looked like, and I was trying to attain that self-created goal! To take it even further, I also judged others based on MY self-created idea of maturity! The joy of the Lord fit within my self-created idea of maturity, but this wild joy did NOT! My soul thought that it was better to be steady than to be unpredictable and out of my mind. When Jesus introduced me to this wild joy, all kinds of triggers (control, religiousness, and my *ideas* of maturity) went off...which meant I could use them for my breakthrough!

CULTIVATING WILD JOY

On the other side of breaking agreement with lies, I ALWAYS have found God to be even better than I had previously known Him. My soul was afraid to lose control and be wildly joyful until I realized that I was in agreement with my enemy. ANY agreement with lies always brings death, and I refuse to let death have any part of me. My rejection of wild joy exposed an area of my soul that still was not convinced of the goodness of God. Even though my soul finds Yahweh better and better with each breakthrough, I didn't have history with Him in THIS area. He is my Healer, Creator, Father, Friend, Lover, and so much more. But I didn't know Him as my Bliss and Ecstasy. When faced with this choice, it was easier for my soul to let go of its fear and control and to choose Jesus in spite of my concerns.

The moment I decided to break agreement with control and choose Jesus, the Heavens split open, and the being of joy finally came! Just kidding, that didn't actually happen. The moment I chose Jesus, I EXPECTED some wildly out-of-control encounter...but that didn't happen. Instead, I saw Jesus with the kindest eyes I have ever seen. He was simply smiling at my soul while it braced for impact. Confused, I looked at Jesus, and without even having to say a word, He answered me. "Jessica, I am safe, and I am kind. I am not going to blow you out of the water. Thank you for choosing my wild joy and for choosing me. Come, and I will help your heart grow its capacity to carry and receive my blissful, divine ecstasy." And that was my introduction to cultivating wild joy. I was SO relieved, and I fell in love with Jesus even more after seeing His kindness to me. He is SO kind and gentle to us.

In this last section, I wanted to give you some keys for cultivating wild joy in your own life.

- Break agreement with judging and rejecting wild joy.
  o Whatever the root is, rejecting and judging things of God will stunt your growth. In my life, control masqueraded as self-control and then flew under my radar because it

was a "fruit of the Holy Spirit." The TRUE fruit of the Holy Spirit does NOT reject or throttle the things of God. If the idea of wild joy offends you, then that is your invitation to take it to Jesus!

- Embrace the foolish things of God.
  - o *1 Corinthians 1:27 (NLT) "Instead, God chose things the world considers foolish in order to shame those who think they are wise. And he chose things that are powerless to shame those who are powerful."*

    As we let go of our self-created ideas of maturity (and let go of control), we become more and more receptive to this blissful, divine ecstasy. YAHWEH uses foolish things, and this wild joy DEFINITELY looks foolish!

- Wait on the Lord.
  - o I can confidently say that your process and journey will look different than you expect. Wait on the Lord, abide in Him, embrace all of Him, and in time, you will experience waves of wild joy.

There are MANY facets to God, so there will be MANY ways for us to engage and experience God! Joy (and wild joy) is just one of the many facets of Yahweh. There will be times and moments of heaviness (where you are plastered to the ground), joy (and wild joy), weeping (over the goodness of God or weeping for others), and many other emotions. He is infinite which means there will be an infinite number of ways we can encounter Him! Life is not all about ONE emotion, facet, or experience. So embrace and pursue ALL of Jesus (foolish things and all). You will find yourself dancing like David danced, turning water into wine, flipping tables, and being out of your mind all while being IN the mind of Christ. Welcome to the realm of pleasures forever more. Enjoy the dance.

Chapter Eleven

CLOSING THOUGHTS FOR THE SONSHIP SERIES

I hope this series has encouraged and inspired you to grow in your relationship with Jesus. Over the course of these four books, we have explored and fleshed out many important facets of being a son of God. My intention was to build a foundation for the burning ones to grow and explore the blissful oneness we have. All of the info in these books is just the basics of the basics. We BARELY scratched the surface of discovering Yahweh and our walk with Him. There is SO MUCH more. Everything I shared in this series goes beyond words. Spiritual things can barely be contextualized by words on a page (including the words in the Bible!). To see beyond our pea-brain, we need spiritual revelation in all things. This can only happen when we intentionally engage with God in a personal relationship, and this is a door only you can choose to go through. Through intimacy and surrender, you will find everything your soul desires, wonderful things beyond what you can ask or imagine, and best of all, you will find the depths and beauty of Yahweh Himself.

There is one final piece that I want to share in closing this book and series. In the "Finding Joy" chapter, I mentioned that my wrong ideas of maturity were exposed. Throughout this series, we have talked *about* maturing, and now I want to discuss it head-on. Maturity is largely subjective from culture to culture, religion to religion, and church to church. And in pretty much all of their definitions, maturity is tied to your ability to proficiently perform the duties/expectations of said group. For this book and personally, I define maturity as the state of not lacking, to be full and complete, with the capacity to carry out whatever you are considered "mature" in.

Unlike culture and religion, God and His ways are NOT subjective. He is the same yesterday, today, and forever. To see past religion's constructs, it is important to ask Jesus what HE thinks and how HE views maturity. I believe that spiritual maturity is the state of BEING who we truly are (and already are) in Christ. Spiritual maturity essentially is finally being out of our soulish mind (*not riddled with lies, wounds, and unrenewed mindsets*) and in the mind of Christ. Here are some examples of what a mature son looks like:

o   Mature sons are a resource instead of a consumer. (We don't need any of the dust on the earth, we are sustained by Heaven!)

o   Mature sons are unshaken in the storms of life. (Circumstances don't shake our confidence in Yahweh!)

o   Mature sons are not threatened by man or demon. (We are one spirit with Yahweh Himself, nothing is a threat to us.)

o   Mature sons embrace the "foolish" things. (God delights in confounding the wise...and we actually enjoy it too!)

o   Mature sons have great power and authority, but they are bridled by self-control and wisdom. (Surrender begets power in the Kingdom, so the most mature sons are the most surrendered ones.)

Unlike physical maturity, spiritual maturity is not about physical age, but heart posture. Stepping back from religious and cultural definitions, ultimately, our spiritual maturity is defined by our capacity to be like our Father. In the Bible, there is a spiritual maturing process or stages laid out. When looking at the Greek text, we can see Jesus mature through these different spiritual stages. Let's take a look...

STAGE 1: Baby [*Nepios or Brephos*]

In Greek, the infant or newborn is *brephos* or *nepios*. Brephos means infant and this is the word used to describe Jesus as a baby. (Luke 1:41, 1:44, 2:12, etc) Nepios can mean infant, but it also means simple-minded or immature person. (*Jesus was never referred to as a nepios, He was only referred to as a brephos infant.*) From what I can tell, there is not a spiritual implication for brephos, but nepios spiritually implies that the person is still very soulish. Remember that man looks at the outward appearance, but God looks at the heart. Even an elderly person can still be a baby in Christ. Nepios is used several times in the New Testament when referring to new/immature believers...

- 1 Corinthians 3:1 (BSB) "Brothers, I could not address you as spiritual, but as worldly — as infants [*nepios*] in Christ."

- Ephesians 4:14 (BSB) "Then we will no longer be infants [*nepios*], tossed about by the waves and carried around by every wind of teaching and by the clever cunning of men in their deceitful scheming."

- Galatians 4:3 (BSB) "So also, when we were children [*nepios*], we were enslaved under the basic principles of the world."

Since Jesus was never referred to as a nepios, it is possible for us to grow out of being immature and soulish. Because of our free will, we can choose to be soulish and immature for as long as we want to...or we can embrace growth and become who we truly are.

STAGE 2: Child [*Paidion*]

The next stage is the Greek word *paidion* which implies a young child. (In the Hebrew culture, this stage encompasses children from around 2 to 12 years old.) Jesus was mentioned multiple times in this stage. (Matt 2:11, Luke 2:21, 2:27, etc) Spiritual "age" does not follow linear time. So the paidion stage spiritually implies someone who is between the irrational infant stage and the discipleship stage. They have matured some, but haven't buckled down to decide to be yielded as a disciple. Here are some examples of the paidion stage...

- Luke 2:40 (BSB) "And the Child [paidion] grew and became strong. He was filled with wisdom, and the grace of God was upon Him." (This verse is referencing Jesus. Notice that even as a child, wisdom and grace were upon Him.)

- Luke 18:16-17 (BSB) "But Jesus called the children to Him and said, "Let the little children [paidion] come to Me, and do not hinder them! For the kingdom of God belongs to such as these. Truly I tell you, anyone who does not receive the kingdom of God like a little child [paidion] will never enter it."

Note: there are not many spiritual maturity references in the Bible at this stage. For the most part, Paul called the believers immature [nepios], disciples [teknon], or mature believers [yhios]. But this paidion stage is a part of the process of maturity, and Jesus is mentioned in this stage.

STAGE 3: Disciple [Teknon]

When believers choose to become a disciple, they enter into the teknon stage. In Hebrew culture, this would be from ages 12 to around 30 years old. After a child [paidion] has their bar/bat mitzvah, they begin apprenticing under a trade and learning adult duties. Again, spiritual maturity does not go in linear time, so this stage is not restricted to a specific age range. Jesus was mentioned in this stage in Luke 2:47-49 when He was teaching at the temple. The teknon stage spiritually implies someone who has chosen to "walk the walk" and submit themselves as a disciple of Jesus. There are lots of teknon references, but here are just a few...

- 1 John 3:10 (NLT) "So now we can tell who are children [teknon] of God and who are children [teknon] of the devil. Anyone who does not live righteously and does not love other believers does not belong to God."

- Romans 8:16-17 (BSB) "The Spirit Himself testifies with our spirit that we are God's children [teknon]. And if we are children [teknon], then we are heirs: heirs of God and co-heirs with Christ — if indeed we suffer with Him, so that we may also be glorified with Him."

- 1 Peter 1:14 (ESV) "As obedient children [teknon], do not be conformed to the passions of your former ignorance"

This is the stage of renewing our minds so that our lives are transformed! When we choose to "walk the walk" with Jesus, we become disciples, and Holy Spirit guides and teaches us all the things we need to know. After we have become discipled and disciplined in the ways of Jesus, we are considered a mature son...

STAGE 4: Mature [Yhios]

In Hebrew culture, once a young man is mature enough to take over his father's business, he is considered a yhios (mature) son. This commonly happens around ages 25-30 years old. In The Foundation (Book 1), we discussed the Hebraic process of "adoption." To recap, when a father decided that his son was mature, he would hold an "adoption" ceremony to present his son to the town and elders as a yhios son. Jesus was called a yhios more than any other stage. The yhios stage spiritually implies someone who has yielded themselves to the Father and now can proficiently live from Heaven and do the Father's business. Here are some of the many examples of yhios sons...

- Luke 3:22 (ESV) "and the Holy Spirit descended on him in bodily form, like a dove; and a voice came from heaven, "You are my beloved Son [yhios]; with you I am well pleased."

- Galatians 4:7 (BSB) "So you are no longer a slave, but a son [*yhios*]; and since you are a son [*yhios*], you are also an heir through God."

- Romans 8:19 (BSB) "The creation waits in eager expectation for the revelation of the sons [*yhios*] of God."

Note: The story of the prodigal son (Luke 15:11-32) is the story of two YHIOS (mature) sons! I was SHOCKED when I found out that both sons were called mature. They were BOTH given their inheritance (verse 12). Later in the story, the older son complains to the father that he was never given even a goat, but the son ALREADY was given his FULL inheritance! Throughout the story, the sons are referred to as yhios sons...until the older son complained about not being given a goat! At that point, the father calls the older son a teknon son because that is how he was acting! (Again, I was shocked. I would have thought the prodigal son would have been called a teknon!) The older son was ALREADY given his inheritance, but he complained to the father as if he had not yet been given the "keys to the kingdom"... sound familiar? We have labeled and taught the story of the prodigal son as if it were about an immature [paidion] son who rejected the father (walked away from the faith), but that is not how Jesus told the story. BOTH sons were mature and missed out on relationship with their father. And BOTH sons didn't walk maturely in their inheritance. There is LOTS to discover and glean from this parable. I hope you ask Jesus about it because this is a very fun parable to explore with Him!

Back to yhios, being capable and mature does not mean we are void of mistakes. Because God is infinite, there will always be infinitely more for us to learn and grow in. We still don't "arrive" ...even at the maturity stage! And guess what? There is one more stage beyond maturity...

STAGE 5: Perfect [*Teleios*]

The final stage mentioned in the Bible regarding maturity IS perfection. This is the *teleios* stage. *"But wait! We can't be* perfect!" Don't freak out. I will explain. Religion adamantly preaches that we will never be perfect because "we're just sinful men." Simply put, this thinking is the doctrine of demons! It is not Biblically supported, so let's explore it! By definition, teleios means: complete, finished, lacking nothing, and perfect. This stage does not exist in Hebrew culture, so it only has spiritual implications. Let's explore some of the verses that reference believers in this stage, then we will flesh it out some more...

- Matthew 5:48 (BSB) "Be perfect [teleios], therefore, as your heavenly Father is perfect [teleios]."

- 1 Corinthians 14:20 (NLT) "Dear brothers and sisters, don't be childish [paidion] in your understanding of these things. Be innocent as babies when it comes to evil, but be mature [teleios] in understanding matters of this kind." [Emphasis mine]

- Ephesians 4:13-14 (NLT) "This will continue until we all come to such unity in our faith and knowledge of God's Son that we will be mature [teleios] in the Lord, measuring up to the full and complete standard of Christ. Then we will no longer be immature like children [nepios]. We won't be tossed and blown about by every wind of new teaching. We will not be influenced when people try to trick us with lies so clever they sound like the truth." [Emphasis mine]

- Colossians 1:28 (BSB) "We proclaim Him, admonishing and teaching everyone with all wisdom, so that we may present everyone perfect [teleios] in Christ." [Emphasis mine]

- James 1:2-4 (ESV) "Count it all joy, my brothers, when you meet trials of various kinds, for you know that the testing of your faith produces steadfastness. And let steadfastness have its full effect [teleios], that you may be perfect [teleios] and complete, lacking in nothing." [Emphasis mine]

There are even MORE verses referencing teleios than what I just quoted, this means we have a strong biblical backing for this concept of becoming complete, perfect, and lacking nothing. If your soul feels resistant to embracing this stage, you can use the trigger as a springboard to transform any religious ideologies left in your heart. Jesus died so we could be complete, perfect, and not lacking! Our healing and redemption are the good news of the gospel! Why would God only heal us partially? Religion has drawn lines where God hasn't drawn any. Religion says "He died to save you from sin, but you can't be perfect. You will always be a fallen man, just barely getting into Heaven because of your incompetence." This is NOT the gospel, and this is NOT found in our Bibles!!

It is SO hard for those of us raised in religion to embrace this idea of a perfection stage of maturity because we have been lied to and kicked down for so long by religion. The crazy thing is that God is so confident in Himself, that He made us, empowered us, and perfected us and it PLEASES Him to do so! God is not insecure and needs to keep us imperfect. Our perfection cannot possibly take away from His perfection and majesty...our perfection actually ADDS to it!! Perfection is NOT bad, and yet somehow religion made us think it is! We CAN be perfect and not lacking anything.

Speaking of not lacking anything, I think this is a good time to expose more of the ideologies of the Tree of Knowledge. The Tree of Knowledge perpetuates the lie that "knowledge" is power and that when we "know" we have "arrived." This perspective perpetuates the lie that we will never be perfect. Adam and Eve were complete and not lacking anything in the garden. Yet in that place of perfection, Eve bought the lie that she was lacking something, just like the older son who complained that he wasn't given "even a goat."

> Genesis 3:6a (BSB) "When the woman saw that the tree was good for food and pleasing to the eyes, and that it was desirable for obtaining wisdom, she took the fruit and ate it..." [Emphasis mine]

Our pea-brain perspective believes that not knowing everything means we are lacking. That is not true! We can be teleios in Christ and still have an infinite number of things to explore and learn BECAUSE Yahweh IS infinite. When we live from the Tree of Life, there is LIFE, abundance, completeness, and perfection in everything we do! Completeness does not mean having all knowledge. Having or not having knowledge is inconsequential.

Throughout this whole series, I have said over and over that our journey is not about arriving at some spiritual destination. Our walk is not about trying to gain "merit badges" and go from one "level" to the next. Remember the marriage analogy. (It is not to be taken lightly because it is one of the ways GOD Himself refers to our relationship with Him!) Marriage is not about the wedding ceremony. Likewise, we don't get married just to die together. The point of marriage is to LIVE with each other and grow in love through the seasons of life. In the same way, maturity is not about attaining a spiritual level as if this life were a video game. That way of thinking is carnal and short-sighted. God is INFINITE so our journey and walk with Him is INFINITE.

The stages of maturity *are* present in scripture, but they are there subtly. There is no formula or map to get from one stage to the next...because "arriving" at a spiritual destination is not the point! In James 1:2-4 (quoted earlier) and in the story of the rich young man (Matthew 19:16-30), we have a clue that surrender and/or hardship help our soul grow. While that IS true that we will mature faster the more we are yielded to Jesus, our soul will still have a process to go through...and that is by design! **Each stage of our maturing process is precious and foundational to our learning to engage with Yahweh and grow as sons.** We definitely to can embrace the process and mature faster, but we will still be on an infinite journey with our infinite God.

Years ago, I had an encounter where I physically smelled burning flesh during a worship service. (For those of you who may have not smelled burning flesh, it is a HORRENDOUS and alarming smell.) Concerned, I immediately scanned the room to look for a fire, and... there wasn't any. I realized that this was a spiritual experience and that Yahweh was inviting me into an encounter. I then turned my eyes to Father God, and I saw myself burning on an altar...it was MY flesh that was burning! Once I got over the shock of what I was seeing, I was able to realize a few things. First, I noticed how precious and pleasing my burning flesh was to Yahweh. It was a FOUL smell...and yet it was a pleasing aroma to my Father because He knew the cost of being a living sacrifice. *(It had been a cry of my heart for my life to be an aroma pleasing to the Lord, and now I saw the beauty and confirmation of that desire.)* The second thing I noticed was that even though my flesh was burning, it didn't actually hurt. I quickly realized that my new creation (me + Jesus) was the REAL me and that only the fleshly and soulish areas of my heart were burning. I was already one spirit WITH the fire, so the only things that could burn were things not of Yahweh. The last thing I observed was the beauty and power of a surrendered life. I was like a phoenix, transformed and one with fire. I was no longer resistant to who I was and who Yahweh was. Surrendered, I was in full agreement with LIFE, and the powerful love of God consumed and became me.

It was beautiful, and I fell in love with Yahweh even more at that moment. Since then, my soul has been in a continual burning process. Layer by layer, the fire is reaching deeper and deeper into my soul. I see now that if I were to be made whole in my soul in an instant, my soul would have never known the faithfulness, patience, and tender love that Yahweh has for me. It is in the day-to-day walking that I see His everlasting faithfulness, kindness, and goodness toward me. Jesus is incredibly intentional with everything He does in our lives and in the encounters we have. Each moment, encounter, and healing is precious in the process.

Even when Jesus was physically here on earth, He didn't cut people's process short. The disciples walked and talked with Jesus in the flesh for three YEARS...and Peter still denied Christ. They fought over who was better and were continually afraid of the bumps on the road. Jesus didn't trump their free will and instantly heal the disciples' soul wounds. Instead, He walked with them day in and day out, revealing the goodness of God and inviting them to step out of the boat. **Anytime we embrace process, we build history with God and build character in our heart. This is why the value of process outweighs the value of instantly being out of pain.** It is through process that these concepts will become your reality. I hope that you are starting to embrace YOUR beautiful process. *Thinking* that God is good is not the same as KNOWING God is good. And the only way to KNOW is by growing history WITH God. Our soul actually needs the process...because in the process, we build history with God. One breath is not enough to sustain us for a whole day or week. The same goes for our relationship with God. One breath of truth, one visitation, is not enough to sustain us. We ABIDE in the Tree of Life, in continual oneness and union with the Father. Even as a mature son and in perfection (teleios), we live in constant and infinite communion that is filled with bliss and pleasures forevermore.

> *Psalms 16:11 (NLT) "You will show me the way of life, granting me the joy of your presence and the pleasures of living with you forever."*

What else is there to say? INFINITELY more. (Pun intended) Thankfully, eternity has been written upon your heart so you can infinitely explore the depths and mysteries of Yahweh. In this entire series, I have been careful with how much and what I shared. I didn't want to spread the table for you...I simply wanted to give you a taste, like an appetizer, so that you would pursue Him and see that He IS good! He has prepared a FEAST for you, and you can go to His table and be full. My hope is that I have given you just enough of a taste to make you hungry and have given you helpful tools to pursue Yahweh.

This is my desire for you...

May you embrace the mystery. Stay humble. Be childlike. Cling to Jesus in all things. Fully surrender yourself on the altar. May you burn until you become the fire. And lastly, when times get hard, remember, the best is yet to come. He has saved the best for last.

It's been a joy and honor to share these books with you,

Jessica Onsaga

I've made up my mind.
Until the darkness disappears and the dawn has fully come,
In spite of shadows and fears,
I will go to the mountaintop with you—
The mountain of suffering love and the hill burning incense.
Yes, I will be your bride.
Song of Songs 4:6 (TPT)

SCRIPTURE PERMISSIONS

Scriptures are quoted from five main translations:

- Berean Study Bible (BSB)
- English Standard Version (ESV)
- New Living Translation (NLT)
- Amplified Bible (AMP)
- The Passion Translation (TPT)

Permissions are as follows:

ABOUT THE AUTHOR

Jessica was a nobody from nowhere, then she discovered she was a son of God! Through the years, she has been on a journey of discovering her identity and growing a personal friendship with Jesus...and now she helps others do the same!

SeraphCreative

Heaven's Heart for Earth

Seraph Creative is a collective of artists, writers, theologians & illustrators who desire to see the body of Christ grow into full maturity, walking in their inheritance as Sons of God on the Earth.

Sign up to our newsletter to know about future exciting releases.

Visit our website :

www.seraphcreative.org

Made in the USA
Columbia, SC
26 July 2025

61032643R00070